WHEN DARKNESS REIGNS: A CAREGIVER'S GUIDE FROM FEAR TO FAITH

WHEN DARKNESS REIGNS: A CAREGIVER'S GUIDE FROM FEAR TO FAITH

WANDA COVINGTON

Published by Tablo

Table of Contents

ACKNOWLEDGEMENTS

It is with great joy and appreciation that I dedicate this book to several special people in my life. First, however, this book would not have been possible without the loving guidance of our Lord and Savior in whom I give all the glory. Second, without the experience of caring for my mother and the extraordinary love and faith that she exhibited, I would not have had the fortitude or knowledge in which to share. Next, I want to recognize and thank my husband, Jim, for his never-ending support and love during those difficult three years. Lastly, but certainly not least, I want to dedicate this book to my brother, David, who relentlessly and lovingly stood by me and assisted me in caring for our dear mother.

INTRODUCTION

Inevitably, dark times will wreak havoc in each person's life without immunity. Struggles and hardships can become overwhelming and debilitating. Among those struggles lie the indelible effects of loss and death. Such tragedies and circumstances can leave one with a feeling of hopelessness. Sadly, loss can be a commonplace experience in the life of a caregiver. Caregiving is a crucial, yet often difficult role given to many who are tasked with providing nurturing and even life-sustaining care for another. Caring for a loved one is a critical responsibility that can ultimately, when intertwined with other complex trials and tribulations, drive a caregiver to become a seeker of answers and strength in order to alleviate pressures from discouragement and even despair. Many who reach perilous levels of desperation are led to search for hope and comfort which is often difficult to find in this fallen world. However, courage to conquer fear and defeat is found in abounding faith and trust that is only derived from seeking the presence and power from a heavenly Father who never disappoints or abandons us in our times of need. The divine Words provided by our Lord and Savior can become a lifeline to those who struggle with life's daunting and crippling challenges. When darkness reigns upon your life, let this writing transform you from being driven by fear and brokenness to one who is abundantly upheld in strength and who overcomes darkness by becoming richly filled with faith.

CHAPTER 1

Encountering Adversarial Attacks

One destiny in life that all will face at some point in time is grief associated with a loss through death. Grief comes to all, perhaps in different forms and in varying degrees but still and yet, it comes. Loss is a very real experience as we travel through this life. Some people seem to be much better prepared to handle these experiences while others become desperately lost and therefore tend to seek a variety of sources to alleviate the anguish that consumes them as a result. Many of these reactions are very real and common human responses in this broken world that we live in today. One keynote to bring forth at the forefront of this writing is to remember this truth; we too will one day experience death and leave this place we call home that exists in the sphere identified as the world. Death tends to be a topic that many people choose to avoid until they are absolutely forced to face it either due to their own pending mortality or that of someone they love. It certainly isn't what most people think of as a pleasant subject to purposely fill their thoughts with on any given day. Assuredly, I acknowledge that the pain that comes with the mental and emotional suffering when death makes its way toward you or the life of a loved one, can be excruciating, terrifying and quite debilitating. My expertise on this matter is simply this; to have loved and lost. My experiences through these losses lead me to the writing of this book with a profound hope that you may share in discovering the source of the hope, strength, and peace that enabled me to endure and persevere through my loss and grief so that you too may attain the same. I speak confidently in saying that the greatest hope to lead you through grueling grief and dark circumstances in life is readily available to you if only you will seek it. Many desperately want it but don't know how or where to begin to find it. My single goal in this writing is to show you how I discovered hope and to be a guide for your discovery of hope in times when darkness reigns.

On average, most people probably never give much thought to actively seeking hope, peace, strength, and comfort as they move along their daily activities in life. After all, our days are generally made up of accomplishing tasks, meeting goals and deadlines, providing for our daily needs, and adding in some recreation when time allows. People tend to live under the perception that self-sufficiency will sustain them, and, on the surface, it appears so. Then the day arrives when an evil adversary enters your life through one phone call. The adversary known as a roaring lion who delivers fear, anxiety, apprehension, and even terror, enters your life through the voice of another person who has called to inform you that a loved one has been taken to the hospital for an unknown medical issue and the tentative test results bear a terrifying diagnosis. Perhaps this adversarial destroyer has held you captive for an ongoing period of time, crippling you almost daily as you watch a loved one deteriorate before your very eyes. It could be that you've been informed by a loved one that they have discovered that they are getting ready to enter a battle for their life against the intruder who came to them unexpectedly and has now forced them to completely reassess their entire life and existence. What if possibly, a person you love dearly has a sudden onset medical event and survives but makes you realize that the destroyer had such a tight clutch on them that they nearly left you forever. Any one of these dark circumstances and many others like them delivered by the great adversary could cripple a person and take them to a pit of despair. My journey to guide you to the way of hope will begin here since it exemplifies the best starting point to reveal how brokenness lead me to wholeness. In the nearly three years prior to this writing, all four of these dark destroyers came into my life in close proximity in time, forcing me to deal with an overwhelmingly difficult amount of challenges, both internally and externally. The roaring adversary was confident he had won. I am sure he was actively planning his victory celebration in honor of my defeat. If there were no hope, this would be a very short writing, however, if you are willing to proceed forward, you will discover that hope is real, it is lifesaving, and it is readily available to you.

For you to have a more complete understanding of the challenges that befell me during those bleak three years, I must give you a brief background of who I was as a person prior to that. For much of my adult life, I served as a law enforcement officer and was approaching the completion of my 25th year of service in January of 2017. That type of career carries its own weights and burdens in and of itself. I managed through those years to move forward in a mindset of self-sufficiency; thinking that I was in control of my life, career, and those things and people connected to it. I had lost my father several years prior and it was my first real experience with loss except for a few friends and a beloved dog. Looking back on my life, those experiences were probably in keeping with the normal progression of time and events in the life of an average person.

After the loss of my father, my mother lived alone in the home they shared for nearly 60 years. She was becoming elderly and health issues were increasingly presenting themselves. In some of the year 2015 and the majority of 2016, I found myself in the beginning stages of, at that time, part-time caregiver to my mother mainly due to some health issues that she had developed, as well as, some early signs of dementia. I was still working a full-time job that required some shift work, a lot of long strenuous hours and a tremendous amount of mental exhaustion from dealing with death and self-imposed human destruction so prevalent in our society today as I was a criminal investigator who also supervised that division in the agency that I was employed by. I was already overwhelmed with a great deal of responsibility that encompassed having control over the fate of other people's lives; a responsibility that I did not take lightly. Consequently, I gave very little attention to my overall health and wellbeing. Having said that, in August of 2016 I learned that my blood sugar test results were abnormal, and I was classified as pre-diabetic mainly due to poor eating habits, lack of exercise, carrying around a little excess weight, and stress. All these shortcomings, I can now look back on and definitively say were directly attributed to the lifestyle of a law enforcement officer in general. But at the time, I moved forward in the way that most people do, within the context of the life that I had defined for myself. I didn't know at the time that I was heading straight for the biggest challenges I would yet face in my life; furthermore, they were the most difficult and painful, and yet ultimately the most rewarding experiences I could have imagined.

Moving into 2016, I had noticed that my mother was having some memory issues, and at first, it really didn't seem significant. She maintained her ability to perform routine daily functions such as cooking, doing her own laundry, grocery shopping, driving and caring for her home. Then some things started to become problematic such as forgetting to pay a bill or not being able to accurately maintain her bank accounts which I later learned to be classic signs of early dementia. Then I noticed small observations such as her forgetting to turn off the stove after making a cup of coffee. I wondered how this could be happening to my mother, a woman I had always seen as a strong, vibrant, and independent person. I was beginning to realize that her living alone was going to present some challenges and extra responsibilities would need to be fulfilled for her to maintain her independence lifestyle. Within the same recent years, she'd had a triple bypass heart surgery and several other vascular surgeries on her neck and legs. She had also turned into a full-blown diabetic. Her specialists were in a city approximately a half hour from her home and some of her follow-up visits were an hour away, so she required someone to take her to those visits because she wasn't comfortable driving in traffic especially in unfamiliar areas. In fact, in time, her ability to drive became a safety issue so it reached a point she didn't drive at all anymore. I knew that her health conditions weren't going to improve much and in fact, some were going to rapidly decline in time. Already being saddled with an immense amount of pressures and burdens from my career which I had spent a lifetime proudly building, the reality was that the gravity of her impending needs was beginning to overwhelm me. I began to wonder how in the world I would ever be able to accomplish all of the things that would be required of me to keep my mother safe and comfortable in her own home and care for her medical needs and maintain my full-time position in my career. I spend a great deal of my allotted vacation time taking my mother to doctor's visits and other such appointments necessary for her wellbeing such as x-rays and testing of various sorts. Mind you, I had to coordinate all of her appointments around my work schedule that included at times unexpectedly being called-out in the middle of the night, scheduled court appearances outside of normal working hours, and a number of other unforeseen occurrences that all came at the expense of the nature of the job. During this timeframe, my mother was inpatient in hospitals approximately 7 or 8 times for various reasons, with one stay lasting up to 41 days. As her dementia became more prevalent, it was necessary to be with her in the hospital most of the time so that sound decisions could be made on her behalf thereby ensuring that she could receive the best care possible. This too required my taking off work to be there. Well, after much soul searching and wrestling with myself and the situation, I finally realized I could not change the fact that she had needs which had to be fulfilled. I also realized that I would have to let go of the career that I had spent a lifetime building in order to be able to give my mother the loving care and attention that she so rightly deserved. You see, I loved my mother very dearly, as I suspect most people probably feel towards a parent. I knew that I would only have one chance to get this right and that this would be the last season of her life and I did not want to miss it. So, on December 31stof 2016, I officially retired from law enforcement at full retirement, with 25 years of service at age 51. Little did I know, I was getting ready to discover some hard truths about myself and many other things in life.

Now that I've presented you with an overview of the circumstances that I faced going into the phase of caregiving for my mother, I recognize that many people in life are facing the exact same circumstances concerning caring for an elderly family member. In fact, according to a publication entitled

Caregiving in the U.S. 2015, "an estimated 43.5 million adults in the United States had provided unpaid care to an adult or child in the prior 12 months." It further stated "the majority of caregivers are female (60%) and they are 49 years old, on average." They go on to say " a large majority of caregivers provide care for a relative (85%), with 49% caring for a parent or parent-in-law" and "on average, they have been in their role for 4 years." Also, it is noted "on average, caregivers spend 24.4 hours a week providing care to their loved one" (The National Alliance for Caregiving (NAC) and the AARP Public Policy Institute, June 2015, Caregiving in the U.S. 2015 – Executive Summary, pp. 9-13). So, what does all that mean for you and for me? It illustrates to me that caregiving requires a lot of work, it is time consuming, and we are not alone in these responsibilities. Somehow there is something comforting about knowing you are not alone. Frankly, I never had the need to research the magnitude of this issue before I was confronted by it, as with many things in life, this is often the case. It didn't necessarily ease the immediate pressures, frustrations, and at times, feelings of desperation, but it did help open my eyes to the thought that if so many others before me had assumed that responsibility and survived, then so could I. You see, each of us are destined to travel a specific path laid out for our lives and whether we learn to embrace it or rail against it can determine how successfully we survive it. So, armed with a little knowledge and a lot of love, I began my walk as a caregiver with only the strength I found in my reservoir filled with self-sufficiency. Time and trials would soon show me that my strength alone was not enough, nor would it ever be enough to help me provide for my mother's needs. You see, my mentality up until that point, was coming from the perspective of a long-time law enforcement officer, which says, I can handle anything and everything with little help from anyone. Flawed at best, but nonetheless, the truth as I saw it at the time. We all bring into any given situation things that are ingrained into our thinking and preconceived notions about how things should or shouldn't be, and so it was with me also. I began to formulate clear and concise strategies to assist me with the functions that needed to be performed thereby giving me a logical and systematic method of organization. Well, in the beginning and through various phases of her care, these strategies were quite helpful, and I plan to include them in this writing so that you may, if you choose, utilize them as well. However, the silent adversary was roaming and biding his time waiting to strike again.

I began the process of adjusting to my new status of being retired and trying to deal with the separation issues that were associated with such changes like the complete disruption of familiar daily routines, a now uncertain definition of self-identification, an unknown sense of belongingness to the larger world structure and a multitude of other emotions that would take a great deal of time to sort through. I later learned these things to be quite normal, though it did not feel so at the time. I never quite felt that I could master one area of my life before another set of challenges was cast upon me quickly and without warning; after all, that is the adversary's strategy. In July of 2017, after having new blood sugar testing, I discovered that I had become a full Type 2 diabetic. So, in August of that year, I decided that I had to make some serious and substantial changes in my life if I was going to ever bring my medical issues under control. I began researching diabetes and how foods affect the body. I made a commitment to begin eating better and decided that since all research was telling me to change eating in conjunction with exercise, I also began to walk a minimum of 30 minutes every other day. I kept a food journal and meticulously logged all foods and beverages I consumed each day to keep up with my nutritional intake and I also logged my physical activities to keep me on track. I had no idea if any of this would work, but I knew that I was predisposed to diabetes since my mother had it and I was seeing in her the person I would become medically if I didn't begin to take this issue seriously.

I suppose up to this point, most of what I was experiencing was merely unfamiliar and even uncomfortable in many ways, but none of it prepared me for what was to come next. During all these new discoveries with myself and with Mom, the second of the four major life events during that three-year span struck our family. Having discovered some physical abnormalities, my sister-in-law sought a medical explanation and it was discovered that she was possibly facing a diagnosis of cancer. Not having quite gained a grasp on the ever-changing circumstances with my mother and the internal struggles I was still dealing with having left my career and facing diabetes, this new discovery felt extremely surreal and I didn't know how to mentally process it. Up until that point in our family, no one had ever faced a potentially life-threatening illness of such magnitude. I found myself searching my mind for anything that seemed rational to explain these findings. I wanted so desperately to offer a solution to make everything normal again because, after all, remember, that's what a law enforcement officer does – find solutions; only I wasn't one anymore and there were no solutions within my control. I was left with a little deeper sense of emptiness and mounting frustration from lack of control. Everything familiar to me seemed to be in a downward spiral and I didn't know how to level it out. Having received the news, my mother always

being the ever-present voice of reason, was the one who
lovingly gave encouragement and reassurance that everything
would be alright. She was always a pillar of strength to
everyone no matter their need. More testing was needed, and
time seemed to crawl in anticipation of the final diagnosis and
what would follow beyond that. During this waiting period,
my mother's dementia was increasing ever so subtly. She just
kept repeating that maybe the tests were wrong and that my
sister-in-law did not have cancer and in fact, said she knew that
she did not have cancer. Perhaps my mother was simply in
denial, which is an understandable response to such impending
news concerning a loved one, but it constantly plagued her
mind almost to a point of obsession. Watching her during this
time, I became vividly aware that my care for her was going to
entail so very much more than meeting physical needs; it was
going to be vital to nurture her mental wellbeing also. I had
begun keeping a journal to document my thoughts and events
as a means of release and was increasingly growing more
isolated from others, consciously or subconsciously, I'm truly
not sure. I began doing whatever was within my means to
keep a tight control over my life so that I could accomplish all
that had been set before me. I became a person driven with a
singleness of mind; to care for my mother and keep my life
from dismantling. I often correlated my feelings at that time in
my life as being trapped in a burning building with no avenue
of escape. But I was soon to learn that I did have the means of
escape and I could challenge that arrogant adversary who so
deviously kept invaded my life.

CHAPTER 2

Acclimating to Crises

Finally, the news came revealing that my sister-in-law did indeed have cancer and in fact, a rare form of it. It is a heartbreaking experience to see loved ones having to face that sort of challenge where the unknown is so unsettling, and the future seems so fragile. Once a treatment plan was formulated, she began chemotherapy and later radiation in hopes of defeating the evil adversary who had unexpectantly chosen her for some seemingly random reason. I wanted so desperately to do something, anything, to bring her and my brother comfort, assurance, and encouragement, but by this point, my self-sufficiency reservoir was running critically low. All the while, my mother maintained her inner strength and positive nature and I was captivated and so internally thirsty for that kind of power and strength. I wondered where it came from and how she could be so resolute in its certainty. I began to intently listen for content and look for the source of her strength. In time, I would come to understand that my mother was providing for me in ways much more valuable than what I could offer her in terms of caregiving. Well, as the year 2017 moved forward, I did my best to adjust to all the changes and unresolved conflicts that seems to shadow me everywhere I went. I had lost all interest in socializing and on at least one rare occasion where I did attend a function, I felt very alone in that room filled with people. I looked around and to be totally honest, I believed that no one in the world had any concept of how depleted and discouraged I felt, nor did I have the energy or words to attempt to explain it. I knew it was no one's fault that they didn't or couldn't understand because frankly, unless I was willing to open myself up to others, there would be no way they could know. It would have sounded very selfish for me to say that it troubled me to see everyone around me carrying on with their normal lives, enjoying themselves in a manner seemingly free from constraints. Though that's what my mind was telling me at the time, I truly did not resent my friends for moving on because a few did try to involve me in gatherings and activities; I just could not function in those environments as the person I had morphed into. I couldn't stop it and I couldn't change it. I felt increasingly helpless. So, I took the easy route and stayed away from people in general unless it involved handling a need for my mother or assisting my sister-in-law if an opportunity arose.

Each new day brought on repetitious duties and intermittently, produced unexpected dilemmas as well. I had come to accept that my routine would involve at least weekly laundry duty, medication management, grocery shopping, and some of the more strenuous housekeeping functions. My mother's legs were increasingly becoming weaker from failed vascular surgeries and a weakening heart condition was taking its toll on her too. But I wanted her to maintain as much of her sense of independence as safely possible so I would let her ride with me to pick up groceries or let her fold the laundry and make the bed. I found that those things were very important to her need to feel useful and productive. I discovered through talking with others in similar situations, with doctors, and in reading a lot of material on this topic, that if I took away all of her responsibilities, even if I was doing it to help her, then she could possibly give up all motivation to do anything because, after all, why would she if someone else was doing it. It was also believed that by keeping her mind active, her thought processes might stay a littler clearer for a little longer. Taking all her normal daily functions away could have led to her feeling a sense of depression and worthlessness. I certainly did not want that, so I found subtle ways to keep her physically and mentally engaged in household functions and activities. She was becoming acutely aware of her physical limitations and even knew that her memory was not as sharp as it once had been. It bothered her and I later heard her say that sometimes she didn't talk because she feared that she would say something that was inaccurate or would be repeating herself unintentionally. Still and yet, her positive outlook remained and was still such an inspiration to me.

Towards the fall of 2017, somehow, I was able to maintain my new eating and walking habits and surprisingly began to lose a little weight, which was also helpful in beginning to curb the diabetes. As I started to feel better physically, I began to also want to discover and define who I was as a person in this new phase of my life. Truthfully, I had long been seeking answers to all sorts of things prior to all of this. I imagine everyone becomes a seeker of such things at varying times in their lives, but my initial seeking came in August of 2009. So, let me take you there just briefly. The one simple decision I made at that time was to merely admit that I knew something was missing from my life and I kept somehow being led in my heart and mind towards understanding how God played a role in my life. You see, my mother was a Christian and I was raised going to church, but as many teenagers and young adults do, I fell away from long-term committed church attendance. I learned the basics in church growing up, enough to know there was more, but not enough to know what the more contained. So, in the few years leading up to 2009, I began to seek the intellectual information on who people said God was and, though much of it was confusing to me, I sought the Bible to see what it said about God. I began listening to and watching different pastors on television and eventually found one, Dr. Charles Stanley, who delivered information about God in a method that made sense to me. Well, I began taking notes when I watched his program and wrote down the corresponding scriptures to match the concepts that he was speaking of. I was learning that there was a lot that I did not know or understand. I was gathering all sorts of helpful scholarly information, but I had yet to make the heart connection. Thankfully, that would eventually come during my three-year dark reign.

As the Fall months approached in 2017, Mom's diabetes worsened, and she began to need two insulin shots per day. Up until that point, I was able to go to her house at non-specific times of the day to check on her and perform the necessary functions for that day, but with the need for regulated insulin, the dynamics of the level of care for her was getting ready to change yet again. Though the shots themselves were fairly simple to administer and my mother said she could do them herself, the reality was that she really could not because her memory had gotten to the point where she was forgetting to take her pill medications on some days so I didn't have the confidence that she would remember to take the insulin shots either. Then she began to hide the left-over pills so I wouldn't know she had forgotten to take them. On occasions, she would self-medicate. For example, she was still able to test her own blood sugars each morning and if the numbers were too high, she would go in the pill box and get an extra dose of the diabetes medication from another day and take that extra pill thinking it would bring the sugar number down to a proper level. This in turn, left one remaining day of the week short a diabetes pill plus her body was reeling from the varying amounts of medications being taken. Once a week, I filled her medication pill box and with approximately 9 pills a day, it became a challenge because some had to be taken only in the morning, at noon, or only in the evening and with her shifting pills around, I began to lose confidence that she was taking her medications properly. She was entering the beginning phases of more frequent doctor's and emergency room visits, and unbeknownst to me at the time, some of those events could have been due to her having access to all of her medications without restricted limitations and taking them inappropriately due to lack of direct supervision. Those types of things had become quite problematic for me because if I tried to hide the pill bottles, she felt as though I was treating her like a child and didn't trust her. It was very painful to think that she felt like I was demeaning her or to think that she felt resentment towards me. The administration of the medication was such a crucial task, I just could not afford to make a mistake. It became a delicate balance in learning how to help her see that the things being done were for her wellbeing. I believe on most days, she truly understood but it was becoming harder for her to accept that her life was changing, and she wasn't in complete control of her own decisions anymore.

While on the topic of medication challenges, I feel it's important to also tell you about the dilemmas of medication refills. As I stated earlier, once a week, I filled my mother's medication pill box which held a 7-day supply. She took approximately on average about 9 pills daily plus the insulin shots twice daily. I was constantly having to make sure that each prescription was refilled and available to put in the pill box so there would never be a lapse of time when she was without them. That may sound like a simple task, but most of her prescriptions had different refill dates. Therefore, I was constantly at the pharmacy picking up prescriptions. Though they were on an automatic refill system, many were never in stock when they were due for refill. I then found myself having to make multiple trips back to the pharmacy to pick up the out of stock medications once they had been filled. All that being said, another issue you may run into deals with your loved one's prescription drug plan through their insurance company. You see, my mother's prescription plan was through a reputable insurance company but the policy was so old that it didn't cover many of the medications she was taking and that left her with a tremendous out of pocket expense that quite frankly, was very expensive for a person on a fixed income. For example, just one of the diabetic medications she was on was almost $800.00 per month that she had to pay out of pocket. With some of the medications, I had to recontact the doctor who would and could in some instances switch the medication to a generic version or one from another class of the medication that was more affordable. However, in order to obtain an updated drug policy with her insurance company, her premiums would have tripled in cost, so the question became whether it was worth paying the exorbitant premium or just pay the out of pocket expense for the medications. Ultimately, we decided to keep her current policy, in part because her medications were always changing, and a new policy wouldn't guarantee coverage of those medications anyway. Then to compound things more, each time that she went to the Emergency Room at the hospital or ended up inpatient, upon her release home, the hospital physician normally changed some or even many of her medications she was normally taking at home. This required that I then reevaluate all the medications she had at home and compare to the new list of medications issued upon release from the hospital and take out the old medicines if they could not be used. I then refilled the box with the new ones only to find that upon her required follow up visit within a week with her regular family physician, he would want her back on the medications she took pre-hospitalization. The whole process became quite a daunting task to say the least and this happened every time she was seen by any number of her doctors.

She had begun to necessitate the need for the services of many types of specialists in her last two or three years of life. In the beginning of that process, some of her doctors were connected with the hospital system closes to her home where she regularly went for appointments. As time went on and after having heart surgery in a larger city in a different hospital network, she needed several other specialists for her health issues. I decided at that time to change her to all specialist physicians who practiced in the same hospital network. Prior to that, the two different hospital systems she frequented, did not have connected computer systems therefore, when a specialist at one hospital needed test results or doctor's notes from the other, it became a complicated and cumbersome process to get all of the information that the doctor needed. Moving her medical needs to the larger hospital, though it was further from home, was by far one of the best decisions made for her overall medical care. Just to give you one example of how vitally important this can be for your loved one's care; my mother had a wonderful vascular specialist at the large hospital. During one of her visits with him, he stated that he believed she needed another vascular procedure to clean a carotid artery. However, he had no idea that her nephrologist at the time was recommending dialysis because both specialists were in two entirely different hospital networks and he had no access to those hospital records. So, if I had not been with her at that appointment to explain to the vascular doctor what the nephrologist had stated to me, he would have, with all good intentions, been ready to proceed forward with setting up a vascular surgery which could have been detrimental to her overall health. But having discovered the information concerning possibly dialysis, he made the decision not to move forward at that time. I learned quickly and early on in being a caregiver that there are some failures in the medical world regarding lines of communication between doctors who have the same patient and yet are affiliated with other hospitals. I don't say that to be critical, I merely mention it because if you are or become a caregiver to someone with extensive medical issues, you will likely run into this sort of challenge and I hope my experience will give you at least one viable solution to explore.

One valuable tool that I developed which I found to be a lifesaver to me, was an information book that I put together and kept with me at all times. The book included the following: my mother's basic information such as address, social security number, date of birth, copies of her insurance and Medicare cards, a copy of her driver's license and a complete updated list of her medications. I also listed her family physician and his office name, address and phone number. I did the same for all her specialists. I had detailed information of her most recent health events and test findings that resulted from them. I kept information on all her health issues and a description of what they were, and the extent of those conditions as had been described to me by her specialists.

Of course, the only way to accumulate this medical information was by being present with her when she met with her specialists. When you do, it is so vitally important to ask questions. I found that a few doctors may seem a little annoyed by that, but most are not. Let me say that even if you experience some who seem annoyed, be persistent, because you are ultimately responsible for your loved one's care and I know you are probably like me in that you want to give them the best loving care possible. I learned that my mother, especially with the dementia issues, was in tremendous need of an advocate because, quite frankly, she could not be that for herself. I watched her during those visits and initially tried to allow her to answer the doctor's questions, but early on, I had to gracefully intervene because when asked of her by the doctor how she was feeling, she would always reply that she was fine and not having any problems, when truthfully, she was having very specific symptoms. Therefore, the doctor was not getting any of the necessary information to accurately assess her situation. It came to the point that she didn't fully understand the questions they were asking, nor did she know what medications she was taking. I ended up having to tactfully explain to the doctors that Mom was experiencing dementia difficulties at which point most of them were patient and caring enough to take a different and softer approach with her, but relied on me for the pertinent information they needed to develop their medical strategies for her care.

These types of situations may make you feel uncomfortable as a caregiver, as it did me, but I knew that in order to accomplish the overall goal of helping her receive the best care she deserved, sometimes I had to be her voice. As it turned out, I had found myself in an awkward position of becoming the mother to my own mother. It was a difficult transition to make, but I'll speak more on the role reversal later in this writing. All I knew at that point in the journey of caregiving for my mother was that life was not going to stop moving forward and I had to decide either I was going to flounder about haphazardly and hope to survive each day or I could start to discover how to find contentment in my situation and perhaps even determine to have peace and find joy in the journey. As you will see through this writing, the decisions we make while on any number of paths we travel in life will have long lasting effects on our hearts and minds perhaps for the remainder of our lives. All I knew at the time was that I wanted, and in fact, needed to make the right choices for my mother and for me. Along the way, in a most wonderful discovery, I learned that I did not have to make those choices alone. I had within me the power to guide my every move and thought, but I just didn't realize it and therefore, I didn't utilize it in the beginning. The crafty adversary had successfully blinded me from this knowledge, but little did he know, I was getting ready to embark on a defense system that could and would disable his ability to destroy me and leave me empty.

CHAPTER 3

Engaging in a Quest for Guidance

I have always been a proponent of education and agree wholeheartedly with the saying that "knowledge is power". I believe that the more we know on a given topic, the better equipped we become at making sound solid choices. So, I found myself wanting to know more about why things were happening in my life so seemingly sudden and of such magnitude. The pressures ushered in by the destroyer kept coming and I knew that I would have to conquer my feelings of frustration and lack of control or they would consume me and would render me useless to my mother. I began to investigate the scriptures for guidance, after all, I proclaimed to believe in God and believe in the Bible, but truthfully at that point, I honestly had never thought about really looking at what God had to say to *me personally*. I always thought the Bible spoke of historical characters and events that happened many years ago and although that's true, I soon learned in a much more personal way that the Bible held all the answers that I was looking for and so very much more. It would be hard to justly condense the treasures I found during my study of what God taught me through my dark reign, but there are many significant scriptures that gave me the solid strength and guidance that put me on a path of healing that I want to share with you in hopes that you too can fulfill your innermost needs.

I want to begin by telling you that I had felt for several years prior that I was being led by something much bigger than myself and I had been slowly growing in my yearning for understanding of God. I had a genuine longing to discover more about God and how I personally fit into His creation. I think we all have some internal need to find out where we fit in the scheme of the world. Having seen so many tragedies while serving in law enforcement, I had already come to the realization that there had to be something much greater than a person's own level of control at work in our world because some things I had witnesses or dealt with had no rational explanation at all. And I thought, if I or anyone else could not have absolute control over circumstances and situations, then what was the point in most of what I did if it wasn't going to make a difference. That would be such a futile way to live and I knew there had to be something else. Little did I know; God was preparing me for the eventuality that was to come; death and grief. The way I began to understand what I was experiencing was to begin by studying specific topics in the Bible. I wanted to see exactly what God was saying to *me*, because I understood that all I had to do was seek Him and I would find Him: "You will seek me and find me when you seek me with all your heart" (Jeremiah 29:13 New International Version). Well, I found myself at a crossroads; either I was going to believe the words of the Bible or I was not. You see, I was at a point of near despair and decided I didn't have much to lose so why not reach out to God and see what happened. After all, if it didn't help me, I'd be no worse off than what I had been *or so I thought*. I knew that if the Bible was the absolute truth as I understood it to be, then I could not pick and choose the parts I wanted to believe. Instead, I must believe it all. Much of it was very foreign to me when I first started studying the scriptures, but as time went on, I found it to offer me genuine solace, solid guidance, and clear instruction for the path that God had put me on. But this did not happen instantaneously. As with many things in life, it takes time to develop the treasures that can end up meaning the most to us like relationships, memories, and trust.

Once I made the solid commitment to discover God, I went to work occupying my free time, when available, to study the scriptures and read them aloud, as my audible voice helped the words become alive to me. I began by specifically looking for scriptures to encourage me to make it through each day. Once I found a passage that seemed to contain those much-needed words, I would read it from the vantage point as if God were speaking those words directly to me, not the character in the Bible it was connected with, *but specifically to me.* Once I learned to do that, I started to faintly begin to feel a tiny refreshment to my soul. For example, one of the passages I studied for encouragement says "The Lord himself goes before you and will be with you; he will never leave you nor forsake you. Do not be afraid; do not be discouraged" (Deuteronomy 31:8). Though the passage in biblical times was encouragement from Moses to the people of Israel and to Joshua that God would be with them, I also know that God's word is timeless and it's translation to me said – The Lord Himself goes before *me*and will be with *me*; He will not leave *me*or forsake *me*. That *I*should not be afraid or discouraged. That had a powerful impact on me because I truly started to understand that God's promises to the people in the Bible were equally meant for me and for you. That to me, is an amazing part of the wonder I experienced as I began to so intently read God's word. So, I pondered this passage and concluded several things.

1. If I believed the Bible to contain words of absolute truth, then *this* passage *must* be true.

2. If the passage was absolutely true and God intended it for *me personally*, then God was directly telling me that He would always be going ahead of me in any situation I may face; He would already be there. He also would be with me and promised that He would not leave me alone to handle any circumstance in that situation. He would *not* turn away from me.

3. If all of this were true, then I could believe that I had absolutely no need to be afraid or discouraged no matter what I faced.

This was a revelation for me because if you remember, I wrote earlier that I had reached near complete isolation from others and had sunk to a painful level of despair. When I read those words written to *me*, I finally began to understand that though I may have humanly felt alone and empty, I was not and in fact, never had been alone. I just didn't know it at the time. You see, the evil adversary had spent a great number of years deceiving me and blinding me from the truth. You may ask me how I knew this specific scripture was true or why I developed such a deep conviction that it was real. Quite simply this; my best explanation would be to tell you that something inside of me started to change. I felt an internal knowing that there was no deception in these words, and they did not feel empty. I felt a strength and belief that perhaps I could handle the tasks set before me in caring for Mom because I was not alone and that assurance, in and of itself, began to quiet my fears and discouragement. For once, I could see a glimmer of hope.

Thirsting to know more, I purchased a Bible concordance

and several books about God's promises. These books directed me to specific scriptures in the Bible according to topics. After all, if I was going to stand upon and gain strength from God's promises, I had to first know what He said. I didn't want to struggle to find scriptures to fulfill my specific needs, so these resources became invaluable tools in my journey. As I was already keeping a journal for other things, I found that writing the scriptures down according to specific topics, helped me to really focus on the actual words and also gave me my own personal quick reference guide to go back to when new difficulties crept into my life or when old ones reared their ugly heads. Countless books are written about the contents of the Bible and certainly on specific topics of the Bible and it would be impossible for me to cover all of the treasured scriptures that came to be a source of my strength but I would like to share those that became invaluable to me. One such passage is "He gives strength to the weary and increases the power of the weak" (Isaiah 40:29). I took that passage and accepted it in its most literal sense because it was though I could hear God telling me personally that He would fill me with strength and power when I thought I could not go on. Well, I had learned enough through the years to understand that God's words are pointless to me unless I decided to accept them through faith. We live in a world filled with skepticism and distrust and truthfully, a long-term career in law enforcement breeds such attributes in a person, as I speak from experience. It is quite an unfortunate by-product of working in the field of criminal justice. So, I absolutely understood skepticism and distrust. However, I reached a point where once I made the commitment to seek understanding of God and His word, I also knew the only way that would work for me was to take that leap of faith. I told myself to just accept God's word at face

value and see what He would do because honestly, up until
that point, everything else in my life made no sense. There's
no comfort in living in between belief and unbelief. There is no
security in wondering if God will be true to me today but not
tomorrow. That form of belief made no sense to me, so I made
a conscious and deliberate decision to absolutely believe God's
word. After all, just because I didn't understand a lot of it yet,
did not mean that it wasn't true. As you'll see later in this
writing, I'm like most believers in that, there are times in life
when I do struggle to understand things that make no rational
sense and do question God, but I've learned this; He doesn't
mind me asking and He doesn't get angry with me for
questioning Him.

By December of 2017, my sister-in-law was in the full
process of her treatments and caring for my mother had
reached a critically new pinnacle. I was then in a routine of
ensuring that my mother was receiving her insulin shots as
prescribed and upon arriving at her home on December 6thto
administer the shot, what I found still haunts me today. When
I entered the home, I immediately saw a pool of blood in the
kitchen and a trail leading into her den. I looked into the den
and found my mother laying on her side and face down on the
floor. I called out to me and she did not answer. I was
horrified, for you see, the very first thought that came to my
mind was that someone had broken into the home and
attacked her. I had lived a great number of years processing
bloody crime scenes and having to witness sights exactly like
my mind was seeing and I instantly reverted to my experiences
as a law enforcement officer. I had never, up until that point
and have never since that moment, experienced the
instantaneous fear and disbelief that came to my mind and
heart in that split second of time. It had always been one of my

greatest fears that something would happen to my mother since she began living alone. However, training and experience quickly called me back into order and upon checking her, she was able to talk and tell me that she had fallen in the kitchen and tried to drag herself to the den where the telephone had been located. Unbeknownst to me at the time, she had fractured her hip and couldn't move to reach the phone, so she laid there until I arrived as she knew I was coming to give her the insulin shot at a specific time. My mother had lain on the floor for approximately one hour and a half prior to my arrival and it breaks my heart to think of that fact even today. But that was the reality of her living situation at the time and is not uncommon for many elderlies to adamantly want to remain in their own homes and not want to depend on anyone else. I had tried on numerous occasions to convince her to wear an emergency medical alert in the event of a fall such as this one, but she never felt like she needed one and therefore refused to allow me to get one. It was a battle I could not win.

She was transported to the hospital and the fracture was such that it had to heal on its own therefore, no surgery was performed. I found myself asking, what more can happen and how will I be able to handle it all? For this writing, I looked back in my journal during that timeframe and I came across a note I wrote on December 16thwhich was shortly after this latest incident. I was still learning how to listen for anything that I felt God was speaking directly to me about and, on that date I wrote that God had revealed to me the previous night the following: I was struggling with having complete trust and faith in God's control and plan concerning Mom's circumstances and my role in caring for her. God told me to start practicing having faith in the small things in life and work my way up to total trust in the big things in life. So, I started doing just that. Each day, I would pray about things that seemed small and insignificant to me in the scheme of life and waited to see how God answered them. Well, I began to notice that, without fail, all of my prayers were answered in such a way that turned out perfectly for the given situation; it may not have been the solutions or methods I would have chosen for the situation, but looking back on each, my solution oftentimes would have probably made things worse or at least not better. You see, God's knowledge is infinite; He knows everything about our lives from before we came into existence until the end of time. How can I compare my knowledge base with that kind of endless wisdom? I can't and honestly, what a relief to me that I don't need to. I came to be comforted by the knowledge that God understood everything happening in my life and therefore, I did not need to understand it; I only needed to learn how to respond to it. One of the greatest assurances I found in God's word regarding this states "Trust in the Lord with all your heart and lean not on your own understanding; in all your ways submit to him, and he will make your paths straight" (Proverbs 3:5-6). Also, encouragement came to me in this declaration - "For my thoughts are not your thoughts, neither are your ways my ways," declares the Lord. "As the heavens are higher than the earth, so are my ways higher than your ways and my thoughts than your thoughts" (Isaiah 55:8-9). The Word was that plain and simple to me, but it certainly was a challenge to change years of ingrained thinking that told me I could sustain myself. God was clearly saying to me that He knows all things; things I would certainly never have the ability or privilege to know on this side of heaven and because of that, He knows exactly how to handle any and every possible situation I could ever find myself in. When I finally realized that I did not have to struggle to always answer the question of why, then I began to feel a freedom within myself that I had never felt. I had spent a lot of my life trying to figure out why some things did or did not happen as I thought they should have to only be left with a feeling of discouragement because the answers just would not come. I now understand that perhaps some things just weren't meant for me to know. I have learned that oftentimes when this happens now, it is because God is asking me to lay aside my self-sufficient attitude and just look to Him and say, alright God, I trust you to handle this fully. Truthfully, the closer I grow to Him, the more I see his faithfulness to me. Imagine that for a moment; God wanting to show me that He is faithful to me. It is an indescribable experience.

I alluded to an adversary earlier in and throughout this writing. I'd like to introduce you to him now. I think we would all agree that there exists in this world good and evil. All we need to do is spend a short amount of time watching the news to confirm this. Well, scripture explains this perfectly; "Be alert and of sober mind. Your enemy the devil prowls around like a roaring lion looking for someone to devour" (1 Peter 5:8). Never doubt that he is seeking to destroy you and me every available chance he can find. But do not be dismayed because James tells us to "Submit yourselves, then, to God. Resist the devil, and he will flee from you" (James 4:7). I have often found myself during my times of darkness speaking aloud to the devil admonishing him to leave and I'm assured through this particular scripture that the devil will flee from me if I will only defy him. Once I learned that I had the power within me to do this, I gained back some control over my life. Even the Apostle Peter goes on to say, "Resist him, standing firm in the faith, because you know that the family of believers throughout the world is undergoing the same kind of sufferings" (1 Peter 5:9).

This tells me that the devil is attacking many of us in all kinds of trials and situations and we are all suffering because of it, but I learned through this scripture that I don't have to allow the devil to have that kind of power over me. What a liberating discovery. Mind you, all these discoveries did not come to me overnight. It was due to a committed effort to learn how to take back control of my life which only became possible once I submitted myself to trusting God and having faith in His promises. You should be aware, however, that God will allow the devil to enter our lives to achieve specific purposes. He will send trials and tribulations to us to accomplish His will and purpose for our lives. Nothing comes into our lives without having first been filtered through God. That's a hard reality to accept and even as a person with faith in and love for God, it can be disillusioning. After all, how can God, who says He loves me, allow me to suffer times of indescribable trials of all kinds? It was only once I found the answers in His word, that I began to start to understand how He works in my life. To demonstrate what I mean, look to scripture in James

"

Consider it pure joy, my brothers and sisters, whenever you face trials of many kinds, because you know that the testing of your faith produces perseverance. Let perseverance finish its work so that you may be mature and complete, not lacking anything (James 1:2-5).

You see, I was learning that God wants what's best for me and because He sees the overall picture of my life, He knows what I will need to experience to become the person He designed me to be. There are things about myself that I would never have discovered had I not suffered various trials in my life and particularly during my three-year dark reign. I was discovering that in order for me to understand how God can and will comfort me, I had to be in need of comfort first by suffering through painful plights or discouraging dilemmas. I also found that for me to experience God's strength, I had to be depleted of my own perceived abilities and acknowledge a state of total weaknesses. Furthermore, I had to come to the realization that though the rest of the world could and often would let me down, God would always prove to be faithful. I was learning these lessons daily as I noted in my journal on December 19th, a prayer that I had spoken to God – Lord, I pray today for wisdom to make the right decisions according to your perfect will. At this time in my life, You have given me the opportunity to be a caregiver to my mother. If You call me to care for her, You will enable me to do it. God was indeed using my sufferings to show me how He also wanted to be my comforter. I didn't realize at the time that God was strengthening me every step of the way. I eventually learned to accept the trials sent to me as blessings because I discovered that God was using those trials to demonstrate His love for me in some way. That too, did not happen immediately. But the truth is that I would never have begun to really know God personally if I hadn't experienced pain and sufferings of many kinds. I thank God daily now that He opened my eyes to the fact that I don't have to fear the unknown or worry when the next trial will surface, and I prayerfully hope that you too will arrive at this reality in your life.

CHAPTER 4

Surviving the Intensity of Helplessness

My mother was still inpatient when Christmas arrived, and I was able to bring her home for Christmas dinner and the opening of gifts before returning her that evening to the hospital. Upon her discharge on December 27th, it was very clear that Mom was no longer going to be able to live alone. Everything in her world and much of mine was getting ready to make a change that would affect both of us for the rest of our lives. I began diligently seeking scriptures that centered on strength. In my journal on December 30th, I wrote the following scriptures on strength and I'd like to share them with you: "But he said to me, "My grace is sufficient for you, for my power is made perfect in weakness" (2 Corinthians 12:9) and "but those who hope in the Lord will renew their strength. They will soar on wings like eagles; they will run and not grow weary, they will walk and not be faint" (Isaiah 40:31). I read those words and really thought about what they were saying to me. I had done a little studying by that point in biblical terminology and the word grace was consistently talked about and I wanted to know more. What I found profoundly affected the foundation of my growing relationship with God: grace is a free gift from God to me as a believer and it is His blessings given to me even though I don't deserve it. In comparison to grace is the term mercy and it is defined as God not punishing me for what I do deserve. So, when I re-read 2 Corinthians 12:9 it had new meaning for me. I realized that because I believed in Him, God loved me so much that He was assuring me that He would bless and strengthen me and that His blessing was all that I needed and I didn't have to do anything other than believe to deserve that blessing. He was clearly telling me that when I am at my weakest, then He can use me the most because I'm not relying on myself or any outside influence; only His love. Therefore, when I discovered in 1 Corinthians 7:17 "Nevertheless, each person should live as a believer in whatever situation the Lord has assigned to them, just as God has called them", I clearly knew what I needed to do. It became so vital, instead of feeling defeated and discouraged and trying to figure everything out by myself, to let God show me how to handle all the details for Mom's care from that point forward. Now that wasn't always easy, and I found myself constantly having to remind myself to turn to God first for guidance because my old ways of thinking kept trying to take over. Furthermore when, even today, I recall in Isaiah 40:31 that "God will renew my strength when I keep my hope in Him, I will feel light in my burdens as though I were soaring on eagles wings, and I will be able to move forward and not be weary"; I am awed by the power in those words. Another scripture that illustrates perfectly what I'm conveying is "The Lord is my light and my salvation; Whom shall I fear? The Lord is the strength of my life; Of whom shall I be afraid" (Psalm 27:1 New King James Version)? This passage of scripture solidified to me that God will lead me and show me the way I should go and that because He gives me strength, there is nothing that I should fear. You see, it is so easy in the beginning phases of a relationship with God to read these words on what I call a surface level and think that they are merely religious sayings, but when you truly stop and deliberately focus on the words and then connect them personally to your life, they take on a whole new and wonderfully transformative meaning.

Well, time quickly approached where a viable solution was needed for alternative living arrangements for my mother. All possible solutions were looked at and as a temporary remedy, a company was hired to stay with my mother during the day and the remaining time was covered by family. The company was employed shortly after her returning home from the hospital and remained in place until she was re-hospitalized for 4 days due to a separate medical issue on January 28thof 2018. Hiring a company to stay with my mother presented its own set of problems which I would like to briefly cover from my experiences here so that you will at least be aware of an outside perspective in case you are ever facing this decision. Let me start by emphatically stating that the following is strictly the experiences I found from one particular home care company. Unfortunately, the company fell short of providing reliable coverage for my mother. There were times when the workers were either late or didn't show up at all. One worker left my mother alone and went to the store. There were some discrepancies in the hours that some of the workers submitted and was paid for versus what they worked. Upon trying to reach the home office to discuss this, I could never get anyone to call me back. The workers were supposed to accomplish certain things like light housekeeping and preparing meals for my mother. The meals were generally made but only one worker fulfilled the list of responsibilities set forth in the contract. On several occasions, I reached out to the person who I initially met with who had advised me to contact her if I ever had a need, and I never got a response back from her regarding any of my questions. In addition to these things, none of the workers were qualified to administer her insulin shots, so I still had to make sure that the shots were given twice daily. The utilization of this company was only intended to be a temporary solution so, after repeated attempts to unsuccessfully resolve these issues, consideration was given to Mom moving from her home into a retirement community in an assisted living apartment. The cost factor alone was a strong influence in this decision. In order to keep my mother living in her own home by utilizing a home care company for only 12 hours per day was twice the amount it would have been for her to move to the retirement community where, in assisted living, she would have around-the-clock care versus the minimal amount and lesser quality of care she received from the home care company. I am confident that there are many competent and reputable companies who provide such services, unfortunately, the company we utilized fell short of my expectations according to the presentation they made to me before they were hired. This unreliability created an increased level of frustration for me because living in uncertainty created a great deal of anxiety and fear.

But life kept moving forward and a discussion with my mother about leaving her home of 60 years and moving resulted in her finally agreeing to go and look at the apartment and facility. One of my mother's greatest fears in moving was that no-one would come to visit her. I tried my best to reassure her that I would always be there for her, but I knew in my heart that uprooting my mother from all things familiar to her, particularly with early dementia, would have a tremendously negative impact. I wanted so very desperately to find some way to keep her in her own home but ultimately, I was not able to find a viable solution. Looking back, I can now clearly see that none of the options I hoped would have happened to keep her at home was a result of the plan that God had already worked out and He merely wanted me to trust Him in the details. After all, remember, faith does require some unanswered questions and I had plenty of them.

Scripture was telling me "For we are God's handiwork, created in Christ Jesus to do good works, which God prepared in advance for us to do" (Ephesians 2:10 NIV). God had already set in motion the direction of the path upon which my mother and I would travel together. It would become the most painful, yet most joyous trip I would ever have the privilege to take in my life. But God did not abandon me at any point in the journey. Rather, I grew confident in God's love for me. I found confidence and reassurance of this when Paul wrote "But the Lord is faithful, and he will strengthen you and protect you from the evil one" (2 Thessalonians 3:3). I thought the evil one had gone dormant from our lives and had moved on finally giving us a reprieve. I was so very wrong.

On February 5th, Mom moved into her apartment in the retirement community. It was a beautiful facility and the staff were very professional and tried to make Mom feel at home from the very beginning. I knew Mom's heart was breaking because she could no longer live her life as she truly wished which was at home in the environment that she was so intimately familiar with. I felt deep inside that she understood her need to be there for the extra care but emotionally, she could not disconnect her longing to still be in her own home. This is a sad reality for many elderlies and a truth that can also tear down the mental fortitude of the caregiver. I suppose in a lot of cases, once a family member moves into a living facility such as this, the role of the caregiver tends to lessen since the staff is there tending to the needs of the loved one. I personally knew that Mom's needs would go so much deeper than just the physical aspect; she would need the presence of loved ones to keep her motivation and willpower strong to help her move forward in this stage of her life. I found that sustaining a life of quality for her was about much more than just attending to her physical needs, it was also about nourishing her soul and spirit, keeping her mind active and alert, and re-enforcing her support system by giving her an abundance of attention and reasons to, not only exist, but also to thrive in the new environment that she had reluctantly consented to move to. The new surroundings, rules and lifestyle changes brought on a heightened level of confusion in her. She became withdrawn and, though she always presented a gracious front to people, at times she became agitated, emotional and even angry. She ran a gamut of emotions that I was not prepared to deal with because I had no previous reference to this type of experience. Every single day presented to me a completely new and unexpected challenge. I found this prayer in my journal during those times that stated, Lord, I pray today giving thanks to You for all blessings that you have given to me. I pray for Your strength today to do the things that you will reveal to me. I pray for a positive mindset this day to find joy and peace even in these difficult times. From my studies of the Word, I noted to myself to always seek God first in all things because if I keep my eyes on Him, He would direct my way. I was just beginning to learn that I needed to change my approach to life and not wait until my circumstances changed to find contentment and even enjoyment. One secret that was becoming clear to me was that I was missing out on the enjoyment that comes from God's promises. You see, I never understood before that God made very specific promises to me in the Bible and He is always faithful to His promises. The following truth is written in Hebrews "Let us hold unswervingly to the hope we profess, for he who promised is faithful" (Hebrews 10:23). But unless I knew what those promises were, there was no way for me to lean upon them or have confidence in them, therefore, I was missing out on a vast amount of joy in life because I was ignorant to all that was available to me.

Somehow Mom and I managed to move forward, advancing through great grief and distress from acclimating to her new living environment. I believe that my mother truly thought that it was a temporary move and that once her health improved, she would be able to move back to her home. I knew, however, because all her specialists were telling me, that her conditions would not improve; only worsen. I wanted to be encouraging to her but found myself constantly trying to redirect her attention to other subjects instead of her idea of going home. It was not an easy task. In fact, nothing had seemed easy throughout that whole process, but I kept reminding myself of the words in Matthew "Come to me, all you who are weary and burdened, and I will give you rest" (Matthew 11:28). I was slowly learning how to grow in my faith in Christ and in doing so, the scriptures took on new and bold meaning to me. God Himself, in His Word was directly telling me to give Him all my worries and in exchange He would give me rest. Oh, how I wanted and needed rest; not just physically, but mentally and emotionally as well. As a typical infant in faith, I would wonder things like why God wanted to take my worries away or want to give me rest and so many other things that I wasn't quite able to understand in its entirety at that point. But I knew enough by then to know that I didn't have to understand everything, I only needed to believe it was true. The following words from the Psalms became a life-calming command from God to me; "He says, "Be still and know that I am God..." (Psalm 46:10). I found that, though it is a simple and short command, it was almost life changing for me. It was simply telling me stop fretting, panicking, worrying, wondering, and fearing things I could not change and just remember that God was in control of all things; therefore, I didn't need to be. Whenever I would feel anxiety rising within me, I would remember that one simple verse and almost instantly, I could feel the calmness sweeping though my entire being. There was no way to explain that feeling other than to know with great certainty that God was keeping His promise to me.

The Bible kept speaking of God's sovereignty. It sounds like a complicated principle, but really it is quite simple. It merely meant to me that God was always in complete control of everything. Now, mind you, I had been a person for many years as a law enforcement officer whose mental makeup was steeped in self-control. How could I ever accept that I really didn't have control over the direction or outcome of events in life? But God's Word makes it quite clear - "... one God and Father of all, who is over all and through all and in all" (Ephesians 4:6). How could I refute this fact and furthermore, why would I want to? With the knowledge that there was nothing beyond God's awareness and that He lovingly and purposefully directs every single aspect of my life, I learned that I could release my fears and anxieties and begin to experience the peace God wanted for me. David's writing in the Psalms reminds me that "The Lord has established his throne in heaven, and his kingdom rules over all" (Psalm 103:19). I believe that David is telling me that God rules over every single detail of my life. I accepted this by faith, and it has literally changed my whole belief system. I give thanks to God for opening my eyes and heart to this reality. I quickly found that it is easy to say that I believe something, but I learned that I'll never really know the depth of that faith until I am challenged to rely upon it. Well, little did I know, the dark reign was about to become even darker and I was going to have to face that challenge head on.

My mother was still in the process of settling into her new apartment when on March 10th, she fell in the bathroom. I received a call from the facility notifying me that Mom had fallen and was being transported to the emergency room at the local hospital. Initially, upon receiving a notification like this, instantly my mind would wonder what the nature of the injuries might be, how extensive they were, how long would she require hospitalization, would she have to receive surgery, how would this affect her dementia, and a thousand other questions that always arose anytime she had an emergency medical situation. I could instantly feel my defensive shield rising and my mind was already mentally developing a plan of self-preservation to enable me to survive this next set of challenges. I hadn't quite learned yet that when a crisis arose like this to first and immediately turn my focus and attention to God because that's where the key to peace and survival is located. I didn't quite understand yet that God was leading me through these events in my life in order to teach me, strengthen me and develop my faith in Him. God, in His infinite wisdom, knew that any plans I might devise to handle the crisis would probably fail without his guidance, because He said in Psalm 94:11 "The Lord knows all human plans; he knows that they are futile." He knew that any plan I developed on my own was going to be in vain. He knew that I needed to understand that He wanted to handle ALL my struggles and trials, not just the ones I wanted to hand over to Him. It was all in His instruction book, the Bible. Clearly, He explains to me in Psalm 32:8 "I will instruct you and teach you in the way you should go; I will counsel you with my loving eye on you." God was, in His perfect timing, showing me how to trust Him in all things and was giving me the strength and courage to move through these difficult circumstances with the assurance that He was there in the midst of the trial with me, guiding me and loving me all the while. I learned that all God was asking of me was to trust and obey Him and step back and watch Him work in my life. Was it that simple? Well, at first, no it wasn't. Because we live in this broken world filled with broken people and corrupt systems, we will always be faced with difficult and trying times in our lives. I know that may sound discouraging, but take heart, it isn't. I'm telling you with great certainty that God can and will enable you to do anything He asks you to do as seen in a scripture known to many "I can do all this through him who gives me strength" (Philippians 4:13). That is absolute truth, but unless you wholeheartedly believe these words written and apply them to your life, they will not work for you. God understands our weaknesses. I know this because it is stated in Hebrews 4:15-16

❝

For we do not have a high priest who is unable to empathize with our weaknesses, but we have one who has been tempted in every way, just as we are – yet he did not sin. Let us approach God's throne of grace with confidence, so that we may receive mercy and find grace to help us in our time of need.

I meditated on this scripture and I believed that God was

saying to me, when Jesus was on earth living life in human form, He faced many temptations, in fact, there isn't a temptation I could ever face in my life that Jesus didn't also face during his earthly life and yet He resisted sin. Therefore, He is intimately aware of any and all temptations that I have and ever will face in my life. Because of that, He understands that at times I will be weak and fail. But thankfully, He goes on to say that God wants me to come to Him boldly and confidently to seek His grace and mercy in these trying times. He wants me to seek His wisdom and direction in all things. It seemed strange to me at first to think that I could boldly go to God. After all, who did I think I was to believe that I could have the audacity to daringly go to God and request anything? I humbly tell you this, through God's grace, I have discovered the answer to the question is this; I am a person who was adopted by God the very moment I accepted and acknowledged the fact that Jesus came to live as a human in this world with the sole purpose of dying on the cross. In doing so, the shedding of His blood symbolically represented the covering of my sins; past, present, and future so that I would never again be separated from God and I was assured that I would spend my eternity with Him in heaven when He called me home. It is important to know that historically in Old Testament times, for a person to be forgiven of their sins, an animal's blood was the sacrifice made to accomplish this. When Jesus came, He became the substitutionary sacrifice, once and for all, for me by shedding His blood which allowed me to become a whole and new person in God's sight. If Jesus hadn't died on the cross on that one day in history, I would never have had the opportunity to have an intimate relationship with God because my sin would always separate me from Him. How do I know this? Romans 6:23 clearly tells me "For the wages of sin is death, but the gift of God is eternal life in Christ Jesus our Lord." All of this made me a child of God who is loved unconditionally, living under the power of His grace and mercy, protected and guided by His wisdom and forever forgiven for any sin that I have ever committed or ever will commit. That is an astoundingly powerful truth and it is the life that I live today. I prayerfully hope you will find your life to be filled with this realization and truth. I hope that the experiences I'm sharing with you in this book will open new insights into this exciting and wonderful life that you too can have.

CHAPTER 5

Seeking Divine Wisdom

As a result of this latest fall, it was discovered that my mother had suffered a broken hip, the opposite hip from her fall in December. By this point, she was extremely tired of procedures, surgeries, doctors, hospitals, and frankly, all things medical. She was very distraught with the news that the hip was broken and that she needed a partial hip replacement. She was 83 years old at that time and the thought of her having to endure another major surgery terrified me. I had heard most of my life that when an elderly person fell and broke a hip, frequently it would result in pneumonia and the person would develop complications which would take their life. I was just not prepared to lose my mother. Again, referencing back to my journal, on March 11th, the day following her fall, I had written Psalm 71:12 which states "Do not be far from me, my God; come quickly, God, to help me." I was slowly noticing that when pressure began to mount in areas in my life, I was beginning to more quickly turn to God's Word for comfort and strength. I was learning that problems and trials would be persistently thrown at me by the devil, but I was now armed with the knowledge that I could resist the temptation to remain in fear and anxiety. As with any situation that comes to us unexpectedly, oftentimes fear and anxiety are a naturally occurring immediate reaction, but the important lesson I was learning, is that it was alright to initially feel those things, but I did not have to live in them. I was beginning to take time to stop and deliberately remind myself that God was in control of all things, He was with me during each trial, and in fact, He was with my mother too. I had never really thought from that perspective up until that point. I realized that God's promises were absolutely meant for me, but they were also equally meant for my mother. I thought all along that I had to assume all the responsibility for caring for her when, in reality, God was caring for her; I was merely in a position granted to me by God to obey whatever He asked me to do.

Well, Mom had been sent to the local area hospital and had to be kept heavily sedated because of the amount of pain she was experiencing. A decision had to be made concerning whether to have the surgery or not due to all her other health issues. She had two choices; one was to not have the surgery and consequently most likely she would have probably been bedridden for the remainder of her life. She would have had very little quality of life and that is not the way she would have wanted to live. The second option was to have the surgery and take all the subsequent risks associated with that such as having a fatal cardiac event or suffering some other system failure during the process which could have ultimately taken her life. It was a hard decision to make. I'd like to take a moment at this point to recommend that before your loved one reaches a medical or mental level where they are unable to make their own decisions about their care, please ensure that all legal documents are put into place concerning the medical wishes they would like. Fortunately, my Mom had the insight to take care of this several years before her initial decline. It was expressly known that my mother did not wish to live her life sustained by medical equipment and that she also did not want to linger around with no quality of life. I had mentioned earlier in this writing about how Mom was such an inspiration to me because of her great strength. I came to completely understand that her source of strength and courage came from her love for and relationship with God. I kept repeatedly hearing my mother say, "God has been good to me" and "God is in control of this."

As her medical and living situations changed over time, she very frequently talked about not being afraid to die. In fact, we had many long conversations about this. She would tell me that she was ready to go whenever God decided to call her home because she was not afraid and she was very excited to see her mother whom she never knew as a child because my mother was four years old at the time of her mother's death. She longed to see her father and all the loved ones who had gone to heaven before her. Her faith was so very strong. It was though at times; I could almost feel it radiating from her. I wanted that. I wanted to be so resolute in my faith that it could not be shaken. After much prayer, a decision was made to go forward with the partial hip replacement because at least there was a chance she would survive and with rehabilitation, she might possibly get back to some level of quality for her life. Thankfully, she was transferred to the larger hospital I spoke of earlier to have the surgery performed by a wonderful surgeon. I spent most every night with her in the hospital because something inside just would not allow me to leave her. There was a small part of me during that time that honestly believed that God was getting ready to call her home. She was so frail and helpless or so it seemed from my emotional perspective. I recall one of the nights I stayed with her; while she slept, I sought out a sermon by Dr. Charles Stanley on the topic of death and heaven and listened to his podcast hoping that in it I could find some new lifeline to cling to in God's Word. It was as if God was clearly telling me that I needed to begin searching His Word for an understanding of death and in doing so was somehow a way for me to start preparing for the eventuality that God would call my mother home. I felt this very strongly and I took this message from God very seriously. So, I set about this new goal to learn all I could about the truth concerning death from God's perspective. I had absolutely no idea at that time the full scope of my need to saturate myself with an understanding of death. I'll cover that in more detail shortly.

Meanwhile, Mom came through the surgery beautifully. It took quite a while for her to regain a normal level of consciousness due to her failing kidney functions which inhibited the anesthesia and pain medications from being readily filtered from her body. Each time she had ever received anesthesia, there was a worsening in the symptoms of her dementia, however, it was a price that had to be paid in order to provide a chance for her to thrive again. After becoming medically stable, she was transferred into a skilled care unit back at our local hospital for physical therapy. On March 21st, I journaled "The Lord is my strength and my shield; my heart trusts in him, and he helps me" (Psalm 28:7). I had further noted that God would enable me to do all that He had called me to do and that I should keep a good attitude and stay in my faith. I felt as though God was continuously telling me to look to that day only and not ahead into the future as shown in the scripture Matthew 6:34 "Therefore do not worry about tomorrow, for tomorrow will worry about itself. Each day has enough trouble of its own." God must have known this was something I needed to work on because while Mom was in rehab, I was worried that she would no longer qualify to reside at her new assisted living apartment because she potentially would not meet the new level of care that would need to be provided because, in assisted living, the resident has to be able to perform some things without assistance. That would have only left an option of putting her in a nursing home and I didn't want to do that if possible. I was to learn that many things I worried about would never come to fruition. They were always needless and pointless worries that God faithfully worked out ahead of time. You may wonder how I learned to focus only on the current day. My best answer would be to tell you that each day I made a deliberate habit of praying to God for his guidance and wisdom just for *that specific day*. I asked Him to help me keep my focus directly on Him. I knew if I stayed focused on Him daily that I would have the assurances from Psalm 16:8 which states "I keep my eyes always on the Lord. With him at my right hand, I will not be shaken." What a beautiful and powerful promise from God.

Meanwhile, while my mother was nearing the last weeks of her rehabilitation, my sister-in-law was still dealing with the evil and insidious cancer that had invaded her. She was so valiant and courageous during all her phases of treatment and I prayed for her daily. I wrestled at times with trying to understand God's will and plan for her life to allow her to have to fight such a battle. Surely, I had no answers to explain that but with absolute certainty, through faith, I did know that God was faithful, He loves His children, He is always with us during our trials, and His plans are always for some good purpose. I, in my human limitations, could not possibly understand what good could come out of my sister-in-law and brother having to enduring this type of personal anguish, but I refused to waiver in my faith that God had everything under control. It reminded me of what Jesus told His disciple Simon Peter concerning his question to Jesus about Him washing his feet. In John 13:7 Jesus replied, "You do not realize now what I am doing, but later you will understand." There are many things that I'll never understand on this side of heaven and I have resolved myself to fully accept that fact. Nowhere is it written or promised to me that God owes me any explanations or that I'm entitled to know and understand everything in this life. But I do take great comfort in trusting in the Lord and believing that whatever comes to me in this life is a result of His unconditional love for me. In this belief, I am left with an unshakable trust that my loving God is at work in my life and in the lives of my mother, sister-in-law and all believers.

Well, I felt as though I was growing by leaps and bounds in my relationship with God by this point and in fact, I was growing more secure and content in the strength and power that He provided to me. I felt like I was certainly going to be able to endure the trying times that had befallen me. One of the things that I've learned through studying God's Word is that He prepares us in stages because He knows how much we can handle at certain times in our lives. Once He helps us navigate through one season of life, we are then able to take on higher levels of trials; all the while leaning on and having faith in His strength and love. What I hadn't yet discovered was that my faith was getting ready to be tested beyond any limit I had yet endured.

On March 31st, while Mom was still inpatient in the hospital, I received a call from my oldest brother's wife who told me that she had taken my brother to the emergency room for chest pains. For clarification purposes, this is a different brother and sister-in-law than the ones spoken of earlier with cancer. Well, naturally, my first concern was that he was going to need some type of heart procedure since heart problems were prevalent in our family's medical history. I was anxious to hear back from her regarding the outcome of his tests. The news came quickly that the test results were tentatively indicating that my brother might have cancer. I recall that moment in my life very vividly; I was in absolute total disbelief that this news could be real or even remotely true. So many things went through my mind in those excruciatingly frightening moments. I immediately prayed to God asking Him to not let this be true. Everything within me was searching frantically for anything that made sense. I kept telling myself that this couldn't possibly be true because cancer did not run in our family. Rationally, I knew that this fact really was no determining factor in a person developing cancer, but I needed something to cling too; some hope that would soothe my aching soul. Slowly, I remembered that I needed to quickly turn my focus back to God. He would give me stability and He would show me the way. I started going back through some of my favorite scriptures, ones that had given me strength in the past, and came back across 1 Corinthians 10:13, where Paul wrote

" "

No temptation has overtaken you except what is common to mankind. And God is faithful; he will not let you be tempted beyond what you can bear. But when you are tempted, he will also provide a way out so that you can endure it.

Certainly, this scripture clearly made me realize that the heartache and desperation I was feeling from this new tragic information was something that millions of people in the world were currently experiencing or had experienced in their lifetime. I began to think about all the people suffering in the world from cancer and other such life-threatening diseases, after all, my own sister-in-law had already been dealing with cancer as well. I asked myself what gave me any right to think that either myself or someone that I loved should be exempt from any such illness. Just because it hadn't happened to me or a loved one up until my sister-in-law and now my oldest brother, didn't mean that it would never happen. I just never imagined it. Upon giving long and serious contemplation to the magnitude and ramifications of how our family would handle the increasingly catastrophic developments with no relief in sight, I made up my mind to just tighten my grip on my faith and pray for God's will to be done. His Word noted above in 1 Corinthians 10:13 told me that He was faithful, and He would not give me more than I could handle, and He would also provide a way out so that I could survive it. As you'll see later in this writing, I have survived it, but I'll also tell you that God never said trials would be easy. There were days that I felt as though I was merely moving in slow motion grasping for hope and comfort from one moment to the next.

Persistence and perseverance became the keys in many ways to my survival during this dark reign. Romans 5:3 says "Not only so, but we also glory in our sufferings, because we know that suffering produces perseverance; perseverance, character; and character, hope." I wondered how I could glory in my suffering and admittedly, it took me a while to understand that, in my life, sufferings must occur for me to grow and mature, becoming all that God intends for me to be. Trials will come to all people. Before all of this, I certainly understood that people experience tragedies in life because I was a firsthand witness to much tragedy in people's lives through my career in law enforcement. Vial wickedness is rampant in our world and so I've never been shocked by disastrous calamities seen in others' lives. But I'll tell you firsthand, those tragedies took on a whole new meaning when they directly began to personally touch my life. I was finding a brand-new perspective on the effects of trials and the lingering consequences of random and unforeseen events and circumstances that can sweep through people's lives. It was easy to fall into a tailspin and lose grip on my hope that I had begun to rely upon so deeply. Well, I turned back to scripture and found these encouraging words I'd like to share; Romans 12:12 "Be joyful in hope, patient in affliction, faithful in prayer" and James 1:12 says "Blessed is the one who perseveres under trial because, having stood the test, that person will receive the crown of life that the Lord has promised to those who love him." I knew with certainty God was telling me to keep moving forward no matter what happened, and He would take care of me. Giving up and falling away from my faith was not an option.

In the aftermath of finding out that my brother's final diagnosis was indeed cancer, I remember thinking how, ordinarily, I would have believed that all the circumstances in my life were completely out of control and on the surface, it certainly appeared that way. I had come too far in my walk with God to turn away from Him and even though, a part of me was indescribably devastated, I knew that I had to stand firm in my faith, or I would not survive these new circumstances and trials. Not only would I have to somehow process this information for myself, but I was also in the position to have to explain to my mother that her oldest son had received a cancer diagnosis. After due and careful consideration on how to approach my mother with this news, I decided that it was best to just be honest with her with the basic facts and not burden her with all the intricate details of the findings. I was discovering with dementia, sometimes the best thing to do is to keep information basic and simple. It leaves less for the brain to have to sort out. Plus, she was becoming very forgetful and I was finding that oftentimes she was mixing up information she had received which made her even more confused and when she became confused, she became very depressed and agitated. I, too, wanted to present the information to her with little emotion because I wanted to minimize the emotional impact that I felt reasonably sure would come. The day came and I sat down with her and told her that he had been to the doctor and they ran test and found out that he had cancer. She was in disbelief and naturally upset, as we all were, but I had prearranged for my brother to speak with her on the phone after I had delivered the news so that she could have the comfort of hearing his voice. Amazingly, as she talked to him on the phone, she exuded a great deal of strength. I realized that her strength was not for herself, but for him. She wanted him to remain strong and I recall her telling him to trust God because He was in control of the situation. I remember her giving him words of comfort and instructing him to follow all the doctor's orders and that everything would be alright. Even amid her own battles, she was still able to be an encourager to others. What an inspiration and a true testament to God. But this was just the beginning of the end for my mother which will become evident as I move forward in this writing.

CHAPTER 6

Discovering the Cornerstone of Strength

On April 13th, my mother was released from the skilled care unit and was accepted back to her apartment in assisted living. God had yet again seen us through another trial and obstacle that was meant to destroy us by the evil one. Prior to my mother's latest medical crisis, she had been able to walk some alone with the assistance of her walker, but by now, she increasingly needed to utilize a transport chair for any long-distance travel; by that I mean even the distance from her apartment to the facility's dining area. My mother absolutely hated the thought of asking anyone to assist her with anything. Many of the things she needed or wanted done, she would wait until my arrival the next day to take care of for her. She was such an independent minded person who didn't want to feel like she was bothering anyone. I tried to explain to her that the staff was there to help her in any way possible. They were so lovingly kind to her. Still and yet, she did not want to imposition them or feel as though they were serving her. As her dementia progressed, some issues became a struggle for us both. Because she knew her memory was changing, she had always asked me to make sure that she was caring adequately for her hygiene because she knew that she might not remember. If you will recall earlier, I stated that I would speak more on the role reversal between mother and daughter, well,

I'd have to say that here is where that really became a painful reality. I never imagined, or frankly had the need to contemplate, how I would feel being in a position to instruct my own mother regarding bathing, dressing, eating and even trying to soothe her mental anguishes much like one would relate to a child. But it happened and it hurt, both of us, I think. But more importantly, it was vitally necessary. To maintain the dignity of her personhood, it was imperative that I tread ever so lightly in my approach to all these sensitive matters. I tried at first to encourage her to bathe in the shower in her apartment and she would insist that she had already had one that morning. I knew that she had not because I had learned little strategies to monitor this by such things as leaving a wash cloth in a certain position and see that it had not been moved from the day before, or checking the soap to find that it was still dry and in the exact position that I left it. Small things like that allowed me to monitor her activities and compare them to the account in her mind. So, I fell into part of my routine with her daily by laying out a fresh set of clothes for her to change into the next day, which she could do by herself on most days. If I did not do this, she would wear her clothes several days in a row. Admittedly, she was not physically active enough to soil the clothes daily but once she got into the routine of changing every day, that really resolved itself. The staff was wonderful about understanding why I was laying out the clothes and they assisted her in the mornings with dressing if she needed it.

Communication, I found, as with most things, was the key to providing Mom with the best care she could have at her new apartment. Whenever a potential issue or question arose, I would bring the information to the supervisors in charge, who were so loving and kind and the matter at hand would always be resolved. They understood my perspective and I appreciated their position which made for a harmonious situation for me and for my mother. It became part of my goal to help Mom acclimate to a routine in hopes of bringing some normalcy to her life. Each day I would arrive and first thing, I would assess her condition for that day. In the beginning, I never knew what I would find when I opened her door. I found myself filling with apprehension and, at times dread, the closer to my arrival at the facility; not dread in being with her, but anxiety because of the unknown. Would I be confronted with her crying and depressed, confused and possibly angry, withdrawn and quiet, or would she be smiling and laughing? I never knew until I breached her doorway and put my gaze upon her face. This became a struggle for me every single day and I went for a period of time in great distress about it. It hurt me enough just knowing that she had to live away from her home, but to know that while she was there, she was experiencing all these varying emotions that I couldn't fix, was almost more than I could bear sometimes. I recalled that I had recently re-read a scripture in my journal that was calling me back to it; John 14: 27 which states "Peace I leave with you; my peace I give you. I do not give to you as the world gives. Do not let your hearts be troubled and do not be afraid." Of course, in this passage, Jesus is speaking of the promise of the Holy Spirit who is given to all believers. I took this passage and thought about all I had begun to learn about the Holy Spirit who I know is a gift from God to me as a believer. He lives inside of me and is the One who provides me peace in times of trouble and uncertainty. He provides me strength and power to endure hardships in times of weakness. He reminded me in this passage that true peace can only come from Him and no other source in this world. Again, I was to lean on the precious promises that God was helping me to understand and showing me how to live out in my life according to His Word.

So how was I to handle this ever-evolving situation became the question I would repeatedly ask myself. But I was talking to the wrong one; I should have been talking to God about it. Once the realization came to me yet again, to turn my focus back to God, I was able to see things much more clearly. I knew that the Bible was God's instruction book for all things in life. Therefore, I set out to see what God might want to tell me concerning the proper way to handle this daily internal battle I struggled with in confronting each new day with my mother. Well, I did find an answer which came to me in Colossians 3:12 "Therefore, as God's chosen people, holy and dearly loved, clothe yourselves with compassion, kindness, humility, gentleness and patience." It could not have become clearer to me if God Himself had appeared in front of me to direct me personally. I was resolutely sure that because I had become a whole new person in Christ when I accepted His death on the cross for me, that God chose me and made me holy and He loved me. He expected for me through this new wholeness to exhibit to others the qualities and attributes listed in that verse. It was though He was directly telling me that regardless of my mother's mindset on any given day, I was to be compassionate, kind, humble, gentle and patient with her. It was such a powerful and dynamic reminder to me that her feelings were more important than my comfort or my struggles. At that moment, I accepted that no matter what each day brought forth, I would humbly accept and support whatever emotion she needed to feel or express during that day. I will readily tell you that this was difficult; not because I didn't intellectually understand that she was experiencing changes physically, emotionally and mentally, but because as a daughter who loved her mother from the depths of her soul, it was agonizing to watch the deterioration and know deep inside that the progression of her ailments would eventually take her away from me. Throughout time, generations of people have cared for their elderly and particularly their parents. Truthfully, I wanted to honor my mother, but I wanted to honor God more. He has very specific commands concerning caring for our parents. I wanted to know exactly what God expected from me as His child and as the daughter to my mother. So naturally, I sought guidance from the one and only source of solid truth; the Bible. There are several scriptures that gave me absolute direction and concrete understanding of my responsibilities in caring for my mother. The first of these scriptures is "But if a widow has children or grandchildren, these should learn first of all to put their religion into practice by caring for their own family and so repaying their parents and grandparents, for this is pleasing to God" (1 Timothy 5:4). Also in verse 8 from the same book and chapter "Anyone who does not provide for their relatives, and especially for their own household, has denied the faith and is worse than an unbeliever." Next, Ephesians 6:1-3

❝

Children, obey your parents in the Lord, for this is right. "Honor your father and mother"- which is the first commandment with a promise –"so that it may go well with you and that you may enjoy long life on the earth.

Also, in Proverbs 23:22, I am told "Listen to your father, who gave you life, and do not despise your mother when she is old." Lastly, in Exodus 20:12 we have this commandment

"Honor your father and your mother, so that you may live long in the land the Lord your God is giving you." Clearly, God was showing me that it was not only His commandment, but my duty to care for my mother; one I chose to do wholeheartedly within the best of my ability with the most love and respect that I had from within the deep recesses of my heart and soul. It was very easy to know my overall goal but knowing how to accomplish it in a manner worthy of pleasing God was a challenge at times. I was to learn that there would come a point in time where surrendering myself totally to God would be the only way I could ever accomplish the tasks that had been set before me. But all things learned are never given in a lump sum therefore, I was still pressing forward making mistakes and fumbling at times but clinging to the saving faith that had brought me thus far. In Philippians 3, Paul wrote about his previous lifestyle of being an unbeliever. His prior life consisted of him persecuting and killing Christians until God brought him, through a series of events, into His loving and saving grace. Even though Paul knew that he had not arrived at the point where he wanted to be in his relationship with and knowledge of God, he knew that he would press on toward the goal of becoming more like Jesus. He illustrated that we should not look back to former mistakes because as a believer, we don't live condemned anymore because God has already forgiven us. He wrote:

Brothers and sisters, I do not consider myself yet to have taken hold of it. But one thing I do: Forgetting what is behind and straining toward what is ahead, I press on toward the goal to win the prize for which God has called me heavenward in Christ Jesus (Philippians 3:13).

Paul, like me, wasn't perfect, nor will I ever be. I was learning each day not to dwell on any past mistakes or failures

I may have made in caring for my mom. Instead, I would choose to keep my focus on the day at hand and keep moving forward in the hopes of running my race successfully. Truthfully, I believe that is all anyone can do; persistently run life's race in a way that will honor God.

As much as I would like to tell you that I handled each new day with grace and dignity, I can't. There were many days during the process of caring for Mom that I experienced many mixed emotions. Things were changing and developing so rapidly, I didn't have much time during each phase of the changes to reacclimate myself before the next change was upon me. I had no resources left except to lean on what I had learned from my loving God and His promises. There were days when I felt as though I was moving along in a stupor or walked about in a state of disorientation. I came to believe that the human mind could only absorb a certain amount of information before sensory overload would shut it down.

Meanwhile, my sister-in-law with cancer had come to a lull in her treatments so she and my brother decided to take some much-needed time away. However, my oldest brother who had only recently discovered that he had cancer was just beginning his journey into the unknown. The mental wear and tear from worrying about her dearly loved family was beginning to take a toll on my mother. She had bouts of crying spells and she often talked about my brother and sister-in-law's cancers with staff after I had left for the day. They would later tell me how she opened up to them and let her emotions flow forth. She would have momentary breakdowns with me as well, but for the most part, I think she tried to stay strong for my sake and contained her feelings for her private moments. I wondered if things would ever be normal again in life, but even then, I didn't know what normal really was supposed to look like. Every time I thought I was establishing a new normal, the parameters that had been set were yet again shattered. I questioned whether I would ever feel carefree and happy and wondered what would have to occur for me to experience it. I had recently studied the topic of happiness as it relates to a believer and rediscovered a well-known scripture found in Philippians 4. In it, Paul describes the secret answer to my question concerning happiness. You see, he didn't speak of happiness; he spoke of contentment. There is a world of difference. I have discerned that happiness is contingent upon my circumstances, whereas, contentment comes only from God. If my circumstances change, so does my level of happiness, which then makes it very unpredictable and volatile. Contentment on the other hand, is a stable fulfilling state of being that only God can provide to me as a believer. In the above scripture, Paul was writing to the people of Philippi from a Roman prison. He tells them

I am not saying this because I am in need, for I have learned to be content whatever the circumstances. I know what it is to be in need, and I know what it is to have plenty. I have learned the secret of being content in any and every situation, whether well fed or hungry, whether living in plenty or in want (Philippians 4:11-12).

How could he be content under those circumstances I wondered? He knew with unequivocal certainty that, as he said in verse 13, "I can do all this through him who gives me strength." Paul knew Christ would strengthen him. His assurances were so strong, he went on to say in verse 19 "And my God will meet all your needs according to the riches of his glory in Christ Jesus." What a magnificent testimony for you and for me. It was as though layers and layers of hidden secrets were being revealed to me through these scriptural discoveries.

Certainly, I had read these words before and as I did so at the time, I visualized how horrible it must have been for Paul to live an existence in a filthy, putrid, dungeon-like confinement filled with vile stench. Even under those circumstances, Paul was able to not only maintain his faith, but he was also able to lift God up so that others could see where his strength came from. I began to examine those passages with a renewed perspective, and I studied it from a personal standpoint. I began to internalize Paul's words and allowed myself to mentally put on Paul's existence. Paul, during his ministry to others, endured great hardships; many were physical that nearly took his life on multiple occasions for the sake of Christ. He knew that his travels on earth were temporary. He knew that as a believer, his citizenship was in heaven and not here on earth as he wrote

"

But our citizenship is in heaven. And we eagerly await a Savior from there, the Lord Jesus Christ, who, by the power that enables him to bring everything under his control, will transform our lowly bodies so that they will be like his glorious body (Philippians 3:20).

Paul wasn't afraid to die, and I felt like when I read of Paul throughout the bible, I was finding through his experiences that I could liken them somewhat to what I was undergoing. If I could make a comparison, it would be to say that, like Paul, I knew I must always pursue the goal that was set before me no matter what obstacles might come. I must also accept that the challenges would most likely be painful and life altering, even to the point of death to self-will. I believe that Paul died to himself and once he did, he realized that it was only at that point that God could come into his life and enable him to continue his ministry. Paul was a strong example of what I needed to become, and he demonstrated the qualities that I needed to embrace to find the contentment in which he rejoiced. I did not want to be fearful of each coming day. I didn't want the circumstances of any given situation to dictate how I would feel. I wanted to be strong and steadfast in my convictions about what I was going to deliberately choose to think and how I would respond to any challenge that may confront me. I was learning that I could decide those things in advance if I wanted to. I learned to predetermine in my mind that, for example, if my mother was having an emotional morning upon my arrival, I could sit with her and comfort her, listen if she wanted to talk, or even read scripture to her from her daily devotional. I could and did tell her that it was ok to cry. By deciding beforehand what actions I might take in any given circumstance for that day, it gave me a sense of peace and direction and allowed me to grasp a new hope in knowing that regardless of the outcome, I could and would be my mother's strength without the fickleness of my feelings and emotions interfering. This new discovery set me on a renewed course leading me towards a higher level of emotional care for my mom. It also helped me to understand that growing in spiritual maturity would not always come easy, but when it came, it was like refreshment to my soul. I had written in my journal that each day is a new day filled with fresh starts and that maturing my faith is a lifelong process. The knowledge that each morning I could awaken to a brand-new beginning with the previous days trials and heartaches long gone somehow gave me new enthusiasm and eagerness to seek the goodness and wonder of God's provisions. In order to embrace this new outlook, I began to set aside all emotional hindrances and made a vow to myself that for the remainder of the time my mother had before God would call her home, I would make each day as eventful and quality-filled as I possibly could and then so many of our adventures began.

CHAPTER 7

Giving Thanks in all Trials

April 17thbrought forth the occasion for me to journal that Mom and I had a fantastic day spent together shopping. I noted that she was laughing and felt good. I gave thanks to God for this blessing. The smallest of blessings were becoming so precious to me by this time. I was learning the importance of giving thanks in all things as seen in God's Word "Rejoice always, pray continually, give thanks in all circumstances; for this is God's will for you in Christ Jesus" (1 Thessalonians 5:16-18) and in Psalm 107:1 – Give thanks to the Lord, for he is good; his love endures forever." I also knew that for me to navigate through these difficult times, I also had to discover God's will for my life and to also change my perspective on some things. My thinking must have led me in that direction as is evident on April 21st when I wrote this prayer to God -God, I ask you to reveal truth to me in every situation in my life and to give me the courage to face it. I then studied the topic of truth in the scriptures to see what God Himself wanted to tell me and He took me to the passage in John 8:32 "Then you will know the truth, and the truth will set you free." Jesus was telling the people of His time to hold on to His teachings because, in His instructions, He would reveal the truth to them about who He was in relation to God the Father. For me, I believed that Jesus was telling me personally to truly seek understanding of His teachings and instructions in the Bible and in doing so, the truth would be revealed to me in such a way that I would not only comprehend it, but would also infuse it into my soul, lean upon it for strength and guidance, and allow it to become the beacon for my life.

Admittedly, by this time, I had become somewhat emotionally stunted and moved about in an almost robotic state of being most of the time. The emotional overload from all of the family dynamics was taking its toll on me and I believe deep inside the recesses of my mind, I subconsciously decided to shut down the part of my psyche that contained anything except the immediate goal of caring for my mother. I had to accept in my heart that regarding my sister-in-law and brother who had cancer, there was absolutely nothing I could do to physically heal them. I knew they both had to walk the path of their own life's journey. I could pray for them and I did so often. Prayer is quite powerful, and I began to rely upon it daily just for strength to make it through each day; even at times, from moment to moment. You see prayer is not a one-sided conversation. It is an open line of communication with the only One who has complete control over every aspect of our lives and who wants to provide for our needs. I have grown to understand that when I pray, God promises that He will hear me if what I am praying for is something that is His will for my life. He gives me the assurance that if He hears me, He will answer my prayer as seen in a writing authored by John

"

This is the confidence we have in approaching God: that if we ask anything according to his will, he hears us. And if we know that he hears us – whatever we ask – we know that we have what we asked of him (1 John 5:14-15).

It was during a growth phase in my spiritual maturity that I began to understand that God's answer to my prayer may not necessarily be the answer I had hoped for, but He is always faithful to answer me according to what is ultimately best for me. I can recall times in my life when I diligently and soulfully prayed for certain things and they did not happen only to discover later in life that, if God had answered the prayers my way, it would have brought about detrimental consequences. God can see my entire existence from beginning to end and He always knows how all the intricate pieces of my life fit together. He loves me so much that He will not answer a prayer from me if He knows that what I am asking for is not in my best interest. The more I study God's Word and learn about His qualities and character, the more I understand how and why He responds to me. I must first know His will for my life, but in order to do that, I must study His Word. I can be confident in God because Hebrews 13:8 clearly states "Jesus Christ is the same yesterday and today and forever." God does not change and furthermore, He cannot lie. This is seen in Hebrews 6:17-19

" "

*Because God wanted to make the unchanging nature of his
purpose very clear to the heirs of what was promised, he
confirmed it with an oath. God did this so that, by two
unchangeable things in which it is impossible for God to lie, we
who have fled to take hold of the hope set before us may be
greatly encouraged. We have this hope as an anchor for the soul,
firm and secure.*

These scriptures gave me the hope that I needed to be certain
that He would always respond to me according to His
principles and promises because He does not change and
cannot lie. In the world we live in today, people, circumstances
and situations are always in flux and are completely volatile.
There are no assurances in that type of uncertainty. With God,
that is not the case. Such a wonderful discovery which restores
a balance to my soul.

As we all know, time stands still for no one and I was
beginning to truly comprehend that time with my mother was
becoming shorter. Her physical condition was deteriorating
rapidly, with intermittent stages of seeming stability. I too
knew that my sister-in-law's condition appeared to be in a
holding phase, with new tests being administered every three
months or so to check the progress of the cancer. Meanwhile,
my brother was beginning treatments for his cancer. My
brother and I had not been close through the years in large part
due to our age differences and life generally taking us in
different directions. I find this to be quite commonplace with
many people. However, after our mother's inpatient
hospitalization in March of this same year, my brother and I
found ourselves both in a waiting room in the hospital one day

and we began talking. Thankfully, from that point forward, we started talking regularly on the phone. After his cancer diagnosis, I knew how vitally important it had become to establish a deeper sibling relationship with him which ultimately turned into a special friendship. I realized, unfortunately almost too late, that oftentimes taking people for granted or not actively pursuing a loving connection with those we care for, can have irrevocable and long-lasting consequences; another valuable and difficult lesson I was to learn. Something within me became almost like a person possessed; driven by a fervent need to spend as much time with Mom as I possibly could and to fill that time with as many activities, experiences, and memories as God would grant us time for. There were days that we were limited by her physical and/or emotional condition, but I made it my sole purpose to keep her active on each day that she felt able. Keeping her active was a fundamental strategy in helping her to concentrate on something other than returning to her home to live, as she never relinquished that dream until the very end. As the month of May approached, Mom's medical condition took on a route of slowed progression giving us both some welcomed stability. I had begun to take my mother to her home for short day trips so she could spend some time with her belongings and maintain her connection to the one place that she felt normalcy. The small things were invaluable to her like touching and smelling her blooming flowers and making a cup of coffee in her own kitchen. Touching her things brought back to her vivid memories of her life prior to age and dementia stealing part of her existence. I would watch her and know inside; her heart was aching to return to the one place that held much of the life she once knew and to find the younger version of the self that she would never be again. She would often tell me, "You never know what your life will be like when you get old". It was heartbreaking to me knowing that I could not grant her the fulfillment of her wish and desire to permanently return home again. I wondered if taking her home for visits was more detrimental than beneficial but, in the end, I had to believe that I had done the best that I could with God's help. Isaiah 41:13 encouraged me with these words "For I am the Lord your God who takes hold of your right hand and says to you, Do not fear; I will help you." I came to rely heavily on seeking God's guidance in all decisions I was making for Mom.

Mother's Day of that year approached and as tradition dictated in our family, we shared a meal at my mother's home. I brought her home and she greatly enjoyed a fish fry that had become one of her favorite types of meals. We had learned that my brother's cancer had metastasized to his spine causing him mobility problems which resultantly necessitated his use of a wheelchair. He and his family came to the Mother's Day celebration and my mother sat beside him during the meal. She was so loving and gentle with him, always encouraging him with her tender words and actions. She put on a brave and strong front around others, but oftentimes as we travelled back to her apartment, she spoke of the sorrow she felt about the trials that cancer had brought to both her son and daughter-in-law. She would become withdrawn at times and exuded a look of deep despair. I would try to remind her of her words to me that God was in control of all things and because He is loving, He must have a special purpose and plan for their trials and hardships. Though we both knew in our hearts that this was absolute truth and accepted God's plan by faith, we also struggled with our human weaknesses which oftentimes longs for an answer to the question of why. I knew in my heart that afternoon on Mother's Day that this would be one of many "lasts" that we would experience together. I tried very hard to steer my focus away from those thoughts and keep them squarely on God first and my mother second. I wrote in my journal on May 13th, the day after Mother's Day, the following scripture – Psalm 29:11 –"The Lord gives strength to his people; the Lord blesses his people with peace." Furthermore, I made a personal note that said - I have learned that it is how I respond under pressure and during times of adversity that help me measure my walk with Christ. Most people can generally present an unassuming demeanor during times of little or no stress in life; it is only when bombarded with pressures and burdens that a person can truly examine themselves to see if they are meeting God's expectations or not. I wanted to be strong for my mother and bring to her the comfort that she so rightly deserved. I felt as though my entire soul seemed to be laid bare for all to see my weakness and shortcomings. I quickly realized that these sorts of thoughts were a mechanism utilized by the devil to distort my thinking and derail me from the path that God had chosen for me. The devil did not want me to rely on God's strength, nor did he want me to believe that I could have peace. However, I had learned enough to know that in order to stay on God's path, I had to quickly correct any wrong or distorted thinking, reassess and fix any wrong behaviors, and get back in line with God's teachings.

In the lull between times of trials, I had begun to take my mother out of the facility as much as possible because I knew it was only a matter of time before another challenge would present itself regarding her physical decline. I had learned that the cancer treatments my brother was taking were making him extremely ill and as a result of his prognosis, he decided to forego the treatments and live the remainder of his life with the most quality he could have in whatever timeframe God would grant him. It was heartbreaking news and even though I had grown tremendously in my faith, I had begun to, yet again, sink into a darkness that was starting to consume and blind me. I was, for the first time in my life, having to face the reality of losing one of my siblings. I was having trouble conceptualizing how that loss would affect my mother's mental stability, how my brother himself would internalize this realization, and how I would part with my brother, who, I had only recently discovered through our reconnection, could also be my friend as an adult. I did not have one single solitary answer. In my journal during this time period, I had written "Have I not commanded you? Be strong and courageous. Do not be afraid; do not be discouraged, for the Lord your God will be with you wherever you go" (Joshua 1:9). His words brought me so much clarity. It seemed as if God came directly down from heaven and looked me square in the eyes and said "this challenge will not overcome you. You have the strength and courage needed to conquer these hardships because I am right here with you every step of the way and I will not let you face it alone." I remember reading the following which was written by a source unknown to me that "difficult times may lead to dark days, but dark days need not mean defeat" (Author unknown). Earlier in this writing I mentioned that I had begun to feel as though God were instructing me to learn more about His Word concerning death because I believed He was preparing me for the eventuality of the loss of my mother. Though that remained true, upon discovering that I was going to lose my brother prematurely, I remembered God's instructions and came to understand that He was leading me to study the scriptures in preparation for the death of my brother as well. I diligently went to work with a passion to discover all that God wanted to show me about death. I am eager to share all those discoveries with you in an upcoming section of this writing. Up until this point, I had always decided to be honest with my mother about all things, at least on a surface level, as too many details would sometimes cause her confusion. I was now having to decide if I should tell her that her son was going to lose his battle with cancer because the treatments were making him ill and they were not going to prolong the disease progression. After much prayer and consideration, I concluded for her well-being not to tell her the newest details of his prognosis because I did not want that to trigger her dementia which oftentimes happened when new and critical information or incidents arose. I felt that it was in her best emotional interest to not burden her with the knowledge that the hope we had held onto was fading and that her son was going to die. I knew that eventually, as time drew near, she would come to understand this fact, but I did not believe she should have to suffer the thought of this every day for an undetermined amount of time. Even at that, I truly believed that deep inside, she understood the magnitude of his cancer and was perhaps processing it internally the best way she knew how.

During the months of June and July of that year, Mom and I stayed very active. Though she had many doctor's appointments, we were able to venture out on her good days. On multiple occasions, I would bring her to my home, and we would have a picnic. We would also go on short shopping trips and have pizza for lunch which she greatly enjoyed. Going out for the day or even only a few hours was somewhat of a challenge on a normal day because Mom could barely walk long distances by that time, so we always had to take a transport chair. I always packed a bag with a few snacks, personal items, and towards the end of our travel times, we would also have to carry oxygen tanks. I always carried a cooler with bottles of water because she became incessantly thirsty from a variety of medical issues. Also, if we were going to be gone for any length of time, I had to arrange to have her medications with me so that I could dispense them while we were away from the facility. So just merely saying we were going out shopping was not always a spur of the moment venture; it always required a bit of pre-planning to accomplish. But after a while, it became like second nature to load and unload all those things. I was determined that nothing would stand in our way of making as many memories as we could and of her receiving the best quality of life that she could have. I just would not settle for anything less. It became increasingly difficult for my brother to leave his home or travel for great distances, so I incorporated into our travels visits with my brother so that he and my mother could spend some time together. She could see at each visit that his physical condition was not improving. She would often ask me after we left if he was getting any better and I would gently respond with, "I don't know Mom, we will have to wait and see." I was emotionally torn in so many directions and was feeling many layers of despair, but I had resolved myself to accept God's plan and cling to His hope. My journaling was a great source of comfort for me as well. It helped me to sort out my thoughts because quite frankly, I had not allowed myself to internalize to my fullest capacity all the tragedy that my family had been dealing with. I would not allow myself to get sidetracked from my sole mission of caring for my mother. I knew a day would come when I would be able to deal with my own personal grief, but that time was yet to come, and I had many hurdles still to cross. I am thankful for my journals because I can look back and accurately help you understand which specific scriptures brought me strength and comfort during each phase of my dark reign. My hope is that you will be able to connect God's Word with the challenges I encountered and discover the strength and comfort available to you in your deepest times of need. Another such scripture I noted on June 18th was "Show me your ways, Lord, teach me your paths. Guide me in your truth and teach me, for you are God my Savior, and my hope is in you all day long" (Psalm 25:4-5). Poignant words reminding me that as long as there is hope, there is life.

CHAPTER 8

Enduring Hopeless Hardship

Towards the end of June, I was specifically being led to write down my experiences and feelings concerning my caretaking role. I felt driven to document how those times were affecting me personally and how God's Word was strengthening, sustaining, and preparing me for her death. I didn't quite understand at the time why that was so important, but I knew it would serve a purpose at some point in my life. In fact, there were few things that I was certain of during those times, but one thing I knew for sure was that God loved me. That knowledge brought me confidence and, in many ways, helping me to realize that I could still find some joy in living amidst the trials. I had noted that because we live in a fallen world, there would be sickness and destruction as a result. Based on what I had learned up to that point, I made a list of instructions that helped keep me grounded and had greatly enabled me to endure the hardships and I'd like to share them with you. They are as follows:

1. Cling heavily to God's love and promises and keep my focus on Him.

2. Do not live in self-pity but be a strong witness to others in my faith so they too may seek to know His love, strength, and comfort.

3. Serve the ill and hurting when I see an opportunity.

4. View these adversities as God seeing me through the heartache and bringing me out more joyful and mature on the other side.

5. Constantly give thanks and praise to God for His faithfulness during this time.

6. Trust that God will not leave or forsake me.

7. Believe that He has put a limit on all my adversity.

8. Understand that this pain and heartache will help me be of service to someone else.

9. Remember that I am not sufficient in my own strength and that none of this is about me.

I would be remiss if I didn't tell you that a part of me had, as a result of my growing frustration, become angry on some levels. I was angry, among other reasons, because I was still experiencing feelings of being out of control. Even though my faith had grown by leaps and bounds, I was still struggling with feelings of weariness and anxiety. There were days when I felt strong and confident in my ability to handle whatever came to me during any given day. But I was still dealing with the seesaw of emotions that took me from steadfast hope to plummets of desperation. I was angry because I wanted to be strong in my beliefs, but I seemed to be fighting a persistent internal battle. I had to constantly remind myself that the conflict I was experiencing was a direct result of the devil himself trying to steal my peace. I knew he was always looking for an opportunity to derail me from my stability. You see, the closer I became to God, the harder the devil was fighting me to keep me distant from the love and truth of God. The devil uses opportunities in times of weakness to attack. Until I understood this, I felt like there was no rhyme or reason to the fluctuating thoughts and emotions that plagued me. But once I realized that Satan was fighting for my soul, only then could I devise a planned strategy to keep from falling into his snares. God's Word speaks a lot about anger and how it is a damaging emotion and response in our lives. I was to discover that I already had the power within me to conquer anger and other such self-destructive behaviors. I felt like God was using these adversities to slowly and methodically chip away at the characteristics within me that did not suit who I had become in my new relationship with Him. In my study of anger, Galatians 5:22-23 revealed that through the power of the Holy Spirit, who came to live within me the moment I received Christ as my Savior, enabled me to have, what the Bible says is the fruit of the Spirit which I have immediate access to. The fruit specifically spoken of is "love, joy, peace, forbearance, kindness, goodness, faithfulness, gentleness and self-control" (Galatians 5:22-23). I sought to understand what all of that meant. I concluded that where there is anger in my life, I can neither produce nor experience the fruit that the Holy Spirit provided that was available to me. There can be no peace and joy when anger exists. I knew I had to find God's remedy to deal with the anger. A key scripture that steered me to the correct response is James 1:19-20 which says "My dear brothers and sisters, take note of this: Everyone should be quick to listen, slow to speak and slow to become angry, because human anger does not produce the righteousness that God desires." It took me a multitude of times reading this passage and failing at controlling my anger before the realization settled within me that, it wasn't enough to merely read the words, it was mandatory that I put them into action. Anger will not be successfully dealt with overnight. For some people, it will take many years and truthfully, without God's intervention, perhaps a lifetime. I can honestly say that I have made great strides in conquering this foe, and I give God all the credit. He has taught be a great deal about patience and self-control; two qualities that I needed improvement upon. He lovingly tells me in Hebrews 10:36 "You need to persevere so that when you have done the will of God, you will receive what he has promised.". I know as long as I live, there will always be an internal struggle between self-will and God's will because I reside in this human body, but I do not have to succumb to defeat because God tells me I am more than a conqueror though Him as told to me in Romans 8:37 "No, in all these things we are more than conquerors through him who loved us." On days when I may have felt weak in my faith, I could rest in the assurance that my feelings were fickle. Thankfully, I am not defined by my feelings and emotions but instead by God's promises.

Thus far, I have revealed to you a gamut of emotions and responses I felt during my dark reign and have made known a variety of strategies and sources utilized during the journey. I feel that you may wonder why it seems that I speak of strength and courage found through God and His faithful Word and concurrently express feelings of despair and weariness. You may ask why the contradiction. The simple truth I discovered is that each phase in our lives will promulgate growth, both emotionally, and hopefully, spiritually. But our growth can oftentimes depend on our willingness to submit to God's plan and the surrender of our own desires, which many times clash with God's desires for us. If we are wise, we will spend our entire lives learning and growing in God's wisdom and love. A simple analogy would be that we wouldn't expect a person to become a doctor without having first given a large part of their life to extensive study and then put into practice all the things they had learned. Then to become a great skilled doctor, they will most likely spend a vast majority of the rest of their career dedicated to perfecting their abilities. As a believer and follower of Christ, it is much the same thing. Faith building, I believe is a lifelong process; one that will certainly require perseverance, dedication and commitment. Prior to the three year reign of darkness that befell me, I, like many people, thought that I understood how to maneuver through life; building a career, developing relationships, calculating the outcome of predicted events, and living my life under the belief that tragedy and heartache always only affected other people. As I grew older, I began to learn of the increased frequency of the terminal illnesses and deaths of acquaintances; something I had never paid much attention to before. Even at that, it still never quite affected me personally until the day that it intrusively invaded MY heart. I had a lot to learn about myself and I wasn't one to just flounder about haphazardly waiting for things to happen. Instead, it was my nature to seek answers and structure my life accordingly. And so, it was; I found myself on a road completely foreign to me, having to retrain my thinking and belief system. It has been one of the most challenging and yet rewarding journeys that I'm still travelling today. And, if I'm smart, I'll never cease seeking and neither will you.

Meanwhile, I was constantly looking for ways to keep my mother active. On days when the weather was inclement or she did not feel up to leaving the facility, we worked on jigsaw puzzles in her room or I would push her around the facility's property, stopping to discuss the many sights of nature's beauty. That may sound very simplistic, but we had many long and meaningful conversations during those times together. I

would take her to play bingo with other residents so she could
socialize with ladies her own age. She enjoyed the arts and
crafts that the facility offered. I would sit with her and assist
her with those crafts because she always seemed more
comfortable when I stayed. Those are moments, even today,
that bring a flood of memories to my mind. I would not trade
that time in my life for anything. I began to relish those quiet
times together because I knew at some unknown point in the
future, her condition would dictate the need for many others
to need or want to be with her and we would no longer have
many days of private time with one another. We took
advantage of all her good days and managed to take several
day trips to different places with historical value. One such
place was a plantation that contained an antique museum.
Many of the items on display were items that were from my
mother's generational era and she absolutely loved seeing
them and discussing her remembrances of them in her own
life. That, in and of itself, made the trip priceless. We made
good memories that day and I have a plethora of photographs
to keep those memories alive. I had begun to take an
abundance of photographs and some videos of my mother
alone and of us together a year prior to her decline. I knew
someday I would want to have the ability to still hear her voice
and see her movement along with images that contained our
memories and time spent together. I'll never know for sure if
all the things we were able to do together really made her life
more fulfilled, but I knew in my heart she deserved everything
within my ability to give her. I believed of all the things I could
offer my mother, the most precious gift I could give her was
my time. In doing so, the remainder of her life was not spent
constantly dwelling on the things she could not do or have
anymore, but on those things that would fill her time until

God came for her. In a way, I felt as though God had tasked me with walking my mother towards her eternal home. As the summer marched on, her medical conditions were deteriorating in subtle but noticeable ways. She had illnesses that caused her body to experience fluid overload, in turn, causing her to have difficulty breathing. Several procedures up to that time were successful at removing the fluid and had bought us a little more time. The reality remained that we were exhausting most, if not all, of the methods by which medical intervention would provide her any relief. I had a certain knowing in my soul that our time together was ending. Indeed, that was to be our last summer together.

In the full swing of summer, my brother who had cancer was taking short trips with his family while he still had enough ability to do so. On July 13th, he and his wife came to visit with me and my mother at her apartment. We spent a pleasant few hours together having lunch and talking as though all things were right in the world. Everything was upside down and nothing felt right. It pained my mother to see her son in a wheelchair after having been such an active person all his life. I watched her interact with him and her mothering instincts were so intense in the way she instructed him to eat properly and follow the doctor's instructions so that he could get well. She was still not aware of the fact that he was discontinuing treatments and that God was preparing his place in heaven. It was hard to know if the dementia was hindering her from fully comprehending the totality of his circumstances or whether she understood deep inside the extent of his illness. Either way, she remained faithful in her trust in God and I believe that is what strengthened her daily. In the meantime, my sister-in-law with cancer and my other brother were spending some much-needed time together trying to sort through the turmoil and chaos that had become their life. Any attempt that I made at trying to rationalize all these happenings only left me empty and devoid of any acceptable reasoning. In general, every day, people experience these types of crises, but it seems to be a rarity to experience these many tragedies at the same time. Change is difficult under the best of circumstances, but these many changes in such a short amount of time was mindboggling. Ultimately, however, when you are faced with having little to no choices or control to rectify or alter the course of events, you must find a way to acclimate. Referencing back to my journals to look for the source of my strength and direction at that time revealed during that July I had written that God is the only One who could help me endure this pain and emerge on the other side of these difficulties with a sense of hope and peace. Psalm 16:8 gave me strength through these words "I keep my eyes always on the Lord. With him at my right hand, I will not be shaken" and comfort in verse 11 "You make known to me the path of life; you will fill me with joy in your presence, with eternal pleasures at your right hand." I believed that God was telling me in these verses that if I kept my focus on Him, He would provide the means for me to handle anything I faced and would show me the way. Not only would He lead me, He would fill me with joy during the journey. In learning how to live from one day to the next, there wasn't much contemplation on how to survive the future. I had yet to learn that I did not have to fear the future because God already lived there. I didn't understand at that point that it wasn't my responsibility to figure out how to plan for the days yet to come. I did ultimately discover through Proverbs 16:9 "In their hearts humans plan their course, but the Lord establishes their steps" that God will show me the way. All I'm required to do is trust and obey Him and He takes responsibility for the rest. With this knowledge came a newfound mindset that prompted the refreshment of my willpower. I am inclined to say that I had not accepted the inevitability that death was raging towards my family to claim for itself two people whom I loved very dearly and there was nothing I could do to stop it.

As I suspected would happen, my mother's condition began to take another decline. She began having great difficulty breathing and along with that, she began to have panic attacks. Her body was again experiencing a fluid overload that required her to be hospitalized in mid-August. To provide her relief, the doctor performed a procedure to insert a catheter into her chest wall. Any medical intervention performed by this time was becoming last resort efforts to maintain her life. The procedure went well and within a few days she was released. The catheter produced wonderful results for her and provided her with a great reprieve for a time period. I noted on August 23rd in my journal that God revealed to me the following: Do not constantly think about my troubles; Focus instead on God and His greatness. I cannot focus on both my troubles and God at the same time. I am to look beyond the current situation to the future. This brings relief to my mind and soul. He reminded me to willingly serve others and to be an example of righteousness. I was to be humble and cast my cares on to God and trust Him. Certainly, these are things that I had read, studied, meditated upon and incorporated into my life over the previous several years, but I still found the need to repeat them time and again in my journal. I had regularly failed miserably in following these words, but I still knew they were true and trustworthy. Therefore, I made it my goal to immediately get back up if I fell away from these principles and start right over because I knew that God was loving and forgiving. He, too, was a God of many second chances. I had been taught through His word that I no longer needed to live in guilt for these types of failures because God no longer condemned me as seen in the promises found in Psalm 34:22 "The Lord will rescue His servants; no one who takes refuge in him will be condemned." So, I could have spent a lot of time feeling defeated and discouraged but instead, I boldly and deliberately chose to view each day as a new and fresh beginning; a clean slate upon which to work and serve the Lord within my abilities.

Towards the end of August and into the first week of September, Mom and I were still able to venture out for lunch and take rides in the country. Her birthday was September 8thand the day before, we began a two-day celebration starting with a trip to her home for another of her favorite meals – a fish fry. The following day we had cake and ice cream at her apartment. I was emotionally torn; I felt so blessed to still have another year to celebrate with her, but I also knew in my heart it would be her last. My brother with cancer had been unable to travel that day to join us in the festivities so I had arranged for her to talk with him on the phone. I still recall listening to her end of the conversation and watching the strength she demonstrated as she talked to him. What should have been a pure and simple celebration of life, also contained a quiet unspoken undertone of sorrow. However, there too was an acknowledgment that God was in control and faith would lead the way. We were unaware at that time that their conversation that day would be the last time she would have the opportunity to speak with him while he was in a conscious state. His condition was deteriorating rapidly, and he was utilizing the services of hospice. Some of the medications used to keep him comfortable were also keeping him in a state of sedation. I had reached the point where I wondered who God would receive into His Kingdom first – my mother or brother. Two days following my mother's birthday, I was faced with the decision of whether to carry my mother to see my brother for the last time. Her dementia and confusion had progressed with these rapidly changing circumstances and I would oftentimes find myself having to retell her information as though she was hearing it again for the first time. I didn't know if it would be more detrimental for her to endure seeing her son near death or just wait and allow her to mourn all at one time when the time came. I knew that the answer would only come through prayer. I reached out to God for guidance, and the One who never fails me lead me to decide that I would take her because I believed that she needed the opportunity to say goodbye to him. Though by this time, my brother was at best in a semi-conscious state, I too felt that he would know she was there, and he would be able to find some peace in her presence. And so it was, we set out on that journey to say our last goodbyes.

CHAPTER 9

Becoming Completely Broken

The trip to my brother's home that day was a solemn ride. My mother was very quiet. I had explained to her that my brother's condition had gotten worse so that she perhaps could somewhat prepare herself for what she was about to see. Everything within me hurt to see the somber look in her eyes and the sorrow upon her face. I knew that she was enduring a pain that no mother should have to experience; the inexplicable agony of the pending loss of a child. I didn't know how to help her. I was at a loss for words. I found that oftentimes, the best comfort I could give her was to remain silent. I knew if she wanted to talk that she would. I recognized this as a time that she needed for personal reflection and to internalize the realities that were to come. Upon arrival, I took my mother in to see him. He was incapable of speech, his eyes were closed, and his body movements displayed a sense of great restlessness. I pushed her chair close to his side of the bed and left them alone giving them some quiet time together in hopes that both would find some closure. She held his hand and soothingly talked to him. It was seen from outside his door, an instantaneous quietening of his inner self as she stroked his hand and quietly cried. The reality had finally come home to her that indeed, her oldest son was going to die. She realized at that point that when she left from that visit, she would never lay eyes on him again until they were reunited in heaven. My heart was literally breaking for her. It would be some time before I could or would allow myself to grieve the loss of my brother. When my mother was ready to leave his side, she did not say goodbye, instead she said, 'I'll see you later.' I did have a chance that day to spend a little time alone with him to tell him that I loved him and that we would meet again one day in God's kingdom. I was empty and numb but knew I had to contain my emotions in order to provide support to my mom. Other family members arrived and, to keep her on schedule, I began the trip back to the facility so she could settle in for the evening. Once in the vehicle and heading back, Mom released her tears and the evidence of her aching soul and brokenness came forth until quietness overtook her. I myself, was too mentally broken and physically exhausted to cry. I was despondent, struggling to move from hour to hour. Finally, I accepted the painful truth that I was soon to lose my brother and newfound adult friend and wondered how all the pieces of our family puzzle would fit together beyond this life changing event.

Not wanting my mother to be alone that night, I decided to stay with her though neither of us were able to sleep. Having dozed a few minutes, I awoke to find my mother sitting quietly on the couch in the dark. I got up and went to her and sat quietly until she began to talk. She kept repeating 'Your children aren't supposed to die before you do.' Again, her tears flowed, and I simply told her it was ok to cry and to feel what she was feeling. After she expressed her emotions, we had the longest and most memorable talk about death and loss. She described to me her readiness to be reunited with her loved ones who had passed away before her; especially her mother, father, brothers, and my father. She spoke of the fact that she was not afraid to die and how God had been so good to her the entirety of her life. We talked about heaven and what a wondrously beautiful place it must be. She knew that when God came for my brother that cancer would no longer have a stronghold on him. In fact, he would never again have sufferings of any kind. She knew deep inside that God was indeed in control of all things and that knowledge alone was a comfort to her and to me as well. Grieving, however, is a process with varying stages that I believe affects each person on an individual basis. She had to find her own way through the grief in a way specifically meant for her. All I could do was be with her and comfort her in any way God would show me.

My mother had lost a significant amount of weight by that time and I knew it would require taking her to buy new clothes for her son's funeral. Even in the couple of days between our last visit with him and the day of his death, she would revert to her thinking that he was going to be healed of the cancer and everything would be alright again. I never tried to argue or persuade her otherwise because, with the dementia, her thinking tended to be confused and irrational at times. I merely attempted to steer her thoughts in a different direction to change her line of thinking. On September 13th, I received the call that my brother's sufferings were finally over. As strange as it may sound, in some ways, I was relieved to know that he no longer had to fight that battle. I had promised my mother that when the time came, I would personally come to deliver the news. I dreaded those 15 minutes of travel from my home to the facility because I did not know how many more times I could endure seeing the pain in her eyes or watch the tears stream down her face. Deep inside, I believed that this news would be the catalyst in destroying my mother's spirit and determination to continue with her fight. We had grown so close over those last two years that I could almost read her thoughts and feel her emotions merely being in her presence. As gently as I could, I brought her the worst news she would experience in her life as a mother; I told her that the Lord had taken him home. Naturally, she broke into tears releasing the excruciating pain she had been dreading. There became a quiet calm within me. I later came to understand that my brokenness had finally overtaken me, and it was at that point I realized I had to give full surrender to God. Once I finally admitted my total helplessness to God, I felt a tender sense of relief invade my soul. It was only then that I realized that God had been waiting for me to reach this point of brokenness so that He could begin the transformation in my life.

To give you an accurate depiction of my thought processes at that time, I again went to my journals. Upon experiencing this total state of brokenness, I noted to myself the following: God permits adversity to force me to do a self-examination. During these times, I see myself for what I really am and not what I pretend to be. Furthermore, Jesus knows that pain sometimes will pave the way for complete healing and restoration of my inner self. I was realizing for the first time that the weaker my internal condition, the greater I would need God. That was part of His goal for my life; to bring me closer to Him in total dependence. He did not want my life to be a daily struggle. Instead, He wanted me to lean on His goodness and love and let Him provide for all my needs. When I finally released every worry, fear, anxiety, and discouragement to Him, I felt a lightness in my soul that I had never experienced before. I was discovering that God's plan was to clearly make known to me exactly what to do and when to do it. He promised to give me personal and specific guidance that would only come from Him through the Holy

Spirit who had come to live within me. I had to allow God to do whatever was necessary to accomplish His goal for my life and not rely on myself. After all, faith is believing that God will do exactly what He promised to me. I was reminded of Jesus' words to His Father in the Garden of Gethsemane before His impending crucifixion "Going a little farther, he fell with his face to the ground and prayed, "My Father, if it is possible, may this cup be taken from me. Yet not as I will, but as You will" (Matthew 26:39). I knew that I too must give total surrender to God's unknown will for my life so that His plan would be accomplished according to His will regardless of the price that had to be paid. The simple truth was that I had to die to self. I made a concrete decision at that point to set my mind on God's assignment for my life and not turn from it. I would simply submit myself to His all-knowing and all-powerful plan with full acceptance of His sufficient grace for anything that I may face in the future. Let me tell you that this wasn't as simple as it sounded. It did put me on a greater and more peaceful path in my life, but I still had to learn that I had to seek His strength daily for the needed persistence in fulfilling His plan and that it was to be a life-long endeavor. You may ask, why bother with the struggle? Simply this – I came to the realization that all alternatives that I could take were nowhere as satisfying as the close relationship that was developing between me and God.

On September 18th, my brother was laid to rest. In a robotic fashion, my mother and I attended the service and thereafter, followed closely behind the hearse as it carried him to his final resting place at the cemetery where he would be lowered in the ground next to my father. She seemed so tiny and frail as we moved her from the vehicle to the canopy to sit with the family. All eyes seemed to be on her, but she never displayed anything except steadfast strength. With God's grace, we made it through the services and after taking her to her home for a short time, she returned to the facility. My birthday was the following day and my husband and I decided to take a couple of days for a brief get-a-way. I had to remind myself that self-care was essential so that I could continue to give her the best of me. The irrational side of me wanted to run as far away and as fast as I could to some remote place where the world could not find me. But running away is never the answer; it only slows down the inevitable. I knew with great certainty that there was still much work to be done in order to accomplish all that God had called me to do. Once I finally became broken from my weaknesses and accepted that I could not handle life in my own strength, then God went to work reshaping my thoughts, beliefs, and priorities. When God started refining and sifting my life to remove all unhealthy hindrances, I started to see that His works began to involve more than just the present-day sufferings; they too revealed other deep-seeded life-long emotions and attitudes that weren't consistent with the life He wanted for me. I realized that I had reached a culmination of toxic learned emotions and thoughts that had developed through life's experiences. Most of my life, I believed that my thoughts and reactions to people and situations were random and unrestrained. It wasn't until I started my walk with God that He began to show me how to live my life with control and purpose. There is a great deal of liberation in that knowledge. He was providing me new skills to employ in my life; to always seek His wisdom, plan how I would handle trials and temptations, wait patiently for His guidance, be careful in choosing my words before speaking, and to keep my emotions in check. God was showing me how to think bigger thoughts and reach for higher dreams in my life. He didn't want me to confine myself to a small existence. He wanted me to understand that, in my mind, I would either triumph or be defeated in my battles.

The month of October was ushered in with this thought noted in my journal – Simplifying my life is one of the best ways to remain peaceful. Oftentimes, I believe the quiet balance in my life was disrupted or the ability for peace to permeate my life was obstructed by the decisions I willfully made. For instance, there were certainly times when confronted by specific issues that I had the choice to either interject myself to resolve the matter or step back and allow God to handle my concern. Pride was the enemy and is a nasty attribute that I suspect some people must deal with on some levels in their lives. I am no different. I found that when I was being prideful, I was saying to God that I could certainly handle that situation way better than He could. But that was never true. I was quickly learning that peace would find its way into my life once I relinquished my perceived right to intervene in every situation that arose. God repeatedly had to correct me until I understood that He wanted to handle everything in my life. All He wanted from me was to trust and obey Him. I was in a newfound training ground that constantly required me coming back to the need of total surrender to God. God wanted to free me from my restraints, and He was the only One who could do so.

Still seeking to keep my mother active, I was still able to take her on some outings during this time. She was increasingly becoming slower in her physical and mental status. But I continued to push forward because the alternative would have contained very little activity in her life outside of four walls. On one occasion, we went to the historical area of Jamestown and spent the day looking at ancient artifacts and

enjoyed discussing the ways of old. Our trip there and back
entailed an experience for her to ride on a ferry across the
James River. Though I believe she greatly enjoyed that day,
she had progressively become quiet and somewhat withdrawn.
I'll never be sure whether her silence was directly attributable
to all the sudden changes in her life and environment, the
dementia, or perhaps a combination of both. By that time, it
truly was a moot point. All that mattered was her happiness
and well-being. I knew that if God was willing, I would one
day be able to reestablish my personal life, but it wasn't yet the
time because this was her season in life to experience as much
as possible, not mine. I was learning how valuable it had
become to embrace every new season and to look for the
blessings in all things, both in positive circumstances and in
difficulties. I had concluded that there were so many things in
life that I had previously set my focus upon that now I realized
had no lasting intrinsic value at all. This was all part of God's
sifting process. He was removing the old and making me new
each day. I had discovered that much of the strength I needed
to move through each day began with a morning ritual of
reading scripture and quiet prayer time with God. I very
seldom missed a morning spent in learning and growing in my
relationship with Him. I can honestly say that my private time
with God changed my life. My day did not feel complete if I
had to forego my connectedness with the only One who had
control over my entire existence.

In the wake of my brother's death, Mom's continual
decline, and the persistent unknowns of my sister-in-law's
cancer progression, I was experiencing a time of great
introspection. I earnestly sought the magical formula to
tranquility during life's storms. There was a blueprint that lead
me to peace and serenity; the truth of the Bible. You see, truth

can't be denied. I knew I had been easily deceived and distracted most of my life by people and worldly things. However, once I began to study God's word with intensity, I found that the solution to everything imaginable was rooted in the truth given by God. That solid truth is what lead me to peace. I was finally comprehending that I did not want happiness as the world defined it; being wealthy, fashionably acceptable, or socially prominent. Instead, I found that contentment was the key because I knew I could be content no matter what was going on around me if I clung to God's love and promises. I did not need great wealth because I knew God would provide for all my needs according to His promises - "And my God will meet all your needs according to the riches of his glory in Christ Jesus" (Philippians 4:19). I no longer had a desire to base my self-worth on acceptance by others because my worth was based on my relationship with God. He loves me for the unique person He created me to be. He said in 1 Samuel 16:7 as He was seeking out David as the replacement king to Saul "But the Lord said to Samuel, "Do not consider his appearance or his height, for I have rejected him. The Lord does not look at the things people look at. People look at the outward appearance, but the Lord looks at the heart." Socially defined prominence was another snare the world would try and use to confine me. But I knew that I had become His child and a co-heir with Jesus Himself and I no longer had a need to prove myself or defend my status. His Word explains this in Romans 8:16-17 "The Spirit himself testifies with our spirit that we are God's children. Now if we are children, then we are heirs – heirs of God and co-heirs with Christ, if indeed we share in his sufferings in order that we may also share in his glory."

On November 7th, I journaled this prayer – Father, help me to always know what is important. Help me to always seek a character that is pleasing to you and not one that impresses the world. Amen. For the first time in my life, I was beginning to believe that I was finally on a thirst-quenching, soul-soothing, and emotionally healing path. It came in God's perfect timing because the storms were on the cusp of raging once again.

On November 8th, upon arrival for my daily visit with my mother, I found her to be experiencing an extreme case of shortness of breath. I was aware that the fluid overload had been building and knew it was only a matter of time before she would again need medical attention for this issue. She was visibly struggling to breathe, and I quickly decided to transport her to the larger hospital where her specialists were located for evaluation. The hospital was notified and once there, an evaluation was completed by the emergency department's doctors. As a result, she was admitted for an inpatient stay. My mother was in the hospital for four days, but the consequence of her deteriorated medical condition dictated the recommendation by her specialist to release her and place her under the care of hospice. These words were crushing to my soul and everything within me fought to accept it. The reality was that there were no further medical interventions that would prolong her life. She was released from the hospital on November 12th, and two days later, she had begun her care under hospice services. She never really understood that her medical status had changed to this degree. I never told her specifically that she was being monitored and cared for under the auspices of end-of-life care because I did not know if she would be fully able to comprehend what that meant. All she knew was that the doctors had said there was nothing else they could do for her. On some level I believed she understood that she was going to die, but she would always say to me that everything was in God's timing and that she wasn't afraid.

What I did notice about myself was this; after these new developments, I felt a strangely controlled calm within myself. At, what should have been the worst yet emotional crisis I had faced in my life, I had expected to become confused, frustrated, angry and emotional. At first, I struggled with this new prognosis. However, once I accepted God's plan for Mom to go on hospice, I quickly turned all those emotions over to Him. In doing so, He brought me such immovable strength and courage, and immeasurable peace and comfort. It truly was an experience that transcended all my human understanding. But remember, after all, that is what He promises us through scripture, and He is always true to His Word.

CHAPTER 10

Developing a Steadfast Focus

The worsening of my mother's condition necessitated the nearly constant use of oxygen not long after she was released back to the facility. It also brought about her need for anxiety medications to calm her when she would begin to struggle with breathing. I knew that once she began those types of medications, she would be sleeping more which, in turn, would lessen our ability to travel or spend time away from the facility. There were days when she still felt good and wanted to get out, so we took full advantage of the time that had become so precious. In the days after her return from the hospital leading up to Thanksgiving, we were able to venture out for a few days on shopping trips and lunch. And as often as possible, she would have surprise visits from my Labrador Retriever, Cody, whom she took great pleasure in seeing. Other days, she would experience extreme tiredness and fatigue. The frequency of incidents with difficulty in breathing was increasing and when they came, I could literally see the panic in her eyes. I knew from the information I had gathered from her specialists that certain organs in her body were in the process of slowly shutting down. She increasingly began to talk about how she missed her father who had to raise her because her mother died when she was the tender age of four. Also, how she longed to see her mother whom she had few memories of.

With the approach of the season upon which to give thanks, another unexpected family crisis arose. While visiting with my mother on the day before Thanksgiving, I received a phone call from a different sister-in-law who told me that another of my brothers was at a local hospital near where they lived and was being transferred to a larger one because he had possibly had a heart attack. The extent of his condition was unknown at that time. I found myself again in a position to have to deliver uncertain and potentially life altering information to my mother. Still freshly reeling from the loss of her oldest son, I was greatly concerned how this news would affect her. I decided to gingerly tell her only the bare minimum to lessen her level of concern until I knew more definitive information. I had begun to learn not to ask what more could happen because I was finding that there could always be something else lurking just around the corner. I was in fact slowly learning to immediately try to accept all things as being God's will for my life. As I did so, it took away the frustration of trying to find the answer to that illusive question of why. Frankly, I believed sometimes it just wasn't meant for me to have that answer. Life became much simpler once I understood this principle. We soon learned that my brother's heart attack had been quite serious. He had coded while being transported to the hospital that day and medical personnel was able to revive him. He was rushed in for a heart catherization where he received stents immediately thereafter. I am thankful to the Lord for sparing my brother that day because I had not been ready to lose another one so soon. With a great deal to be thankful for, the next day was Thanksgiving and I took Mom to her home for a family dinner as we had done my entire life. That year was so very different having lost my oldest brother to cancer and another brother unable to be there due to his hospitalization. With my mother now being on hospice, the thought of that being our last Thanksgiving together brought many somber thoughts and emotions to me. I was experiencing a raw acceptance that I never had the occasion to encounter before. Having most of the family together that day brought about a vague sense of familiarity and normalcy to life that was quite short lived. I found myself pondering the concept of thanksgiving and what that meant for my life. Certainly, it was a time to give thanks for all things, but until recently, I had not truly understood how much I really had to be thankful for. I was discovering that God's Word directed me to always express my thankfulness to God as seen in Ephesians 5:19-20 "… Sing and make music from your heart to the Lord, always giving thanks to God the Father for everything, in the name of our Lord Jesus Christ.". Sometimes I found it hard to feel thankful for the trials I had and was experiencing, but the secret to that was understanding that feelings are fickle. Just because I felt one way did not necessarily make it my reality. I knew that when emotions clouded my thinking, it was nearly impossible to see or acknowledge the truth that God was trying to reveal to me through those trials. The key to enduring such hardships was to keep my focus entirely on God and seek His daily guidance in all my thoughts, actions, and attitudes. It wasn't an automatic reaction to seek Him; it was a habit that I had to consciously learn to develop. As with all habits, it takes time to break them and time to develop them. Therefore, if you find yourself in this situation, don't be too hard on yourself. Instead accept it as part of the learning process of growing in a relationship with a loving God who only wants what is best for you. I made a concrete decision to absolutely trust God even when I didn't understand His ways.

By this time, I had begun to experience enough of God's grace, mercy and answered prayers to be assured that indeed, He would respond to my requests in a way that would best meet my needs. As I learned to flourish in my knowledge and wisdom of who God is, I realized that I had been living my entire life to fulfil only those things that would meet some internal desire I had for myself. It took me quite a while to comprehend that my life was not meant to be lived solely for myself, but to do the will of God. That may seem and sound internally stifling, but it became one of the most liberating decisions I ever made. You see as I spiritually matured, I was able to see that my old self-desires were racked with unhealthy and often detrimental choices. Once I turned my decision-making over to God's will, it became much easier to navigate through each day because I did not have to rely on my own devices to find self-fulfillment. God was graciously providing for all my needs and began to show me the utter futility in my previous longings and desires.

After the Thanksgiving dinner, while driving my mother back to her apartment, I couldn't help but notice how frail and exhausted she appeared. She was becoming increasingly withdrawn and quiet, perhaps partly due to the dementia related confusion. Also, excessive amounts of noise and stimulation had become too overwhelming for her. But mostly I believe she was developing a calmness in her spirit. The totality of the events from that previous year and a half had taken a devastating toll on her, not only physically, but also mentally, and emotionally. But the one thing that never faltered was her undeniable faith in our loving and ever-present Heavenly Father. Oftentimes, I would just watch in awe at the strength and confidence she exuded no matter the circumstances. She never complained about her physical pain or the mental anguish that must have plagued her soul. She had unwittingly helped me to understand that inner personal pains and torments do not have to spill out onto others around me just because they exist; only one of many powerful life lessons she instilled in me.

The latter part of November afforded us the opportunity to go on a couple of excursions that entailed lunch and shopping for the upcoming Christmas season. By then, I had perfected my abilities to pack a travel bag with anticipatory items of need for the day. I became very skilled at loading and unloading a transport chair and oxygen tanks. It was almost second nature by that point. In many ways, I was walking through life with a very narrow focus, not steering from the mission straight in front of me within each day. I was reminded of a scripture found in Proverbs 4:25-27 - "Let your eyes look straight ahead; fix your gaze directly before you. Give careful thought to the paths for your feet and be steadfast in all your ways. Do not turn to the right or the left; keep your foot from evil." God was very clearly instructing me to keep my focus first and foremost on Him and He would guide me through each day and enable me to maneuver through any snares the devil may have set before me. This scripture, and many like it, became so much more than just words on paper; they became a lifeline to me. They gave me strength, encouragement, and the assurance I needed to, not only survive each day, but to also find joy and peace amidst them. Much of my life, I believed the Bible was a collection of elusive words and teachings meant for other people. It was only when I comprehended that those same words were meant specifically for me that a whole new world opened to me. Only then did my life began to be enriched by its awe-inspiring and life-giving power.

A rare opportunity presented itself on December 6th. I had

previously arranged to take my mother on that date to visit one of the homes she grew up in as a young girl. The home had been restored and made into a bed and breakfast filled with beautiful antiques and furnishings. It also had been listed on a historical landmark registry. The current homeowners had opened the home as part of a Christmas tour of historical homes and an article had been written about the tour in one of our local newspapers. Having discovered the article, my mother saved the paper and with great enthusiasm showed everyone who came to visit her. I knew without hesitation, that I had to make that trip happen. It had been many years since she had last been inside the home and I wondered if she would truly remember having lived there. Though she remembered the outside of the home from the picture in the paper, once we arrived and went inside, her memories were vague and disconnected; except for one brief moment. In that one flash in time, she had a wonderful recollection of memories that involved her and her youngest brother sliding down the stairway from the second story. I captured that moment of clarity in a photograph of her pointing up the staircase with a child-like expression of innocence in her eyes and a beaming smile on her face. As she recanted that memory, I knew that even though that may have been her only solid remembrance, it made the whole venture worthwhile. As we moved from room to room, I wondered what she must have been like as a child. I had never given much thought to the person she used to be before she grew into the woman who became my mother. Age had taken so many things from her by that time; her mobility, clarity, dexterity, and memories among other things. But the things she never lost was her ability to remain steadfast in hope and faith and the resilience of having survived a life riddled with hardships and trials while still maintaining great dignity and grace. I was learning that age could not take captive the essence of who a person truly becomes.

Meanwhile, my brother was recovering from his heart attack and came to see our mother as quickly as was feasible in an effort to show her that she did not need to worry about him. He knew that in her fragile state of mind, she would need to physically see and talk to him before she would be at ease. My sister-in-law's condition seemed to be holding steady with her recent test results indicating that the cancer had not moved or grown. There is something to be said for the old adage that says to count your blessings. I was finding it to be extremely important to acknowledge and profess my appreciation for the blessings still to be found during that three-year dark reign. Though darkness had tumultuously swept through our lives in such a way as to seemingly consume our souls, strength was still to be found in God. After all, from my viewpoint, there was only two choices – trust in God or struggle. I did not want to give in to the battle that raged inside of me. God had talked in His Word about the method by which a believer should approach battles. He spoke through His servant Paul who stated

"

Put on the full armor of God, so that you can take your stand against the devil's schemes. For our struggle is not against flesh and blood, but against the rulers, against the authorities, against the powers of this dark world and against the spiritual forces of evil in the heavenly realms. Therefore put on the full armor of God, so that when the day of evil comes, you may be able to stand your ground, and after you have done everything, to stand.

Stand firm then, with the belt of truth buckled around your waist, with the breastplate of righteousness in place, and with your feet fitted with the readiness that comes from the gospel of peace. In addition to all this, take up the shield of faith, with which you can extinguish all the flaming arrows of the evil one. Take the helmet of salvation and the sword of the Spirit, which is the word of God (Ephesians 6:11-17).

If you would, envision a soldier who gears up to prepare for engagement in a battle. To prepare himself, he places upon his body an assortment of specially designed clothing, footwear, and apparatuses that will increase his odds of survival during the midst of combat. Believers in Christ are metaphorically no different. We live in a fallen world where Satan seeks to destroy us through the decay of sin. Each of us live in a combat zone where the attacks often come through things like deliberate deceptions, intentional barrages of emotional assaults, painful personal encounters, and consequences of poor life choices. However, God never intended that we should engage in these battles unprepared. Instead, He equips us with all the armament that we need to victoriously conquer our opponent. We are assured victory when we know the truth found in God's Word and then allow His Word to guide our every action to do what is right. We know that we are to have faith that God will accomplish for us what we cannot do for ourselves. We are to cling to His promises and stand strong in the face of challenges with complete confidence that God is at work defending and protecting us from harm and evil. I slowly learned to equip myself daily with God's protective gear so that I did not have to constantly expend all my attention and energies in fighting battles I could never win on my own merits or in my own strength.

The joyous Christmas season began its approach. I wanted to keep the traditions as close to normal as possible. One of the things that always brought back fond memories was decorating the Christmas tree with Mom. Knowing with some degree of certainty that this would be the last Christmas I would spend with her, I decided to take her home for a day of tree adornment. I took out all the decorations and ornaments and placed them before her. Many were collected through the years; some having originated by the crafty hands of her children and grandchildren. Certain ones she could remember fashioning by crocheting them into the shapes of snowflakes during her more youthful years before arthritis had stiffened her fingers. Among them were glittered designs of stuffed felt material that were representative of the season such as a snowman, a Christmas tree, a holly leaf and a bell. Those found a special place in my heart because I could vividly recall the day in my childhood when we made those together. It was a bittersweet experience being there finding enjoyment in a lifelong ritual that would never again be a part of my life after that day. More importantly, Mom appeared to take pleasure in the revival of those old memories, but I knew that she too understood that life had become and would continue to be forever different.

During the following weeks just before Christmas day, Mom and I did not leave the facility much because she had weakened, and her breathing had become problematic. We managed to have lunch at the restaurant on the premises and still shared good quality time together in her apartment on the days that she was not struggling. We played Bingo or other games, worked puzzles, and watched movies. I had given her a Kindle on which to do word search puzzles. She was not familiar with such electronic devices but after a brief lesson, she found great enjoyment in finding the words. It seemed to keep her mind active and her attention diverted from the daily routine that had become her life. She quite frequently fell asleep sitting up while we watched movies or as she worked the digital puzzles. It had become painfully evident that her body was winding down. It hurt me to watch her decline even to the point that I felt like I was prematurely grieving her death. I discovered there is such a thing called anticipatory grief found in situations where death is impending; oftentimes it is found in situations where there is a long-term terminal illness. I did some reading on that topic and it somehow soothed me to know that it was a real experience and that many others had travelled that path before me. It was comforting to know I had not been alone. There is a lessened sense of isolation in discovering that, even though I may not have personally known many of the people grieving in that way, just knowing they existed helped to validate the crippling emotions that oftentimes I felt.

Earlier in this writing, I mentioned I believed I was being led by God to begin preparing myself for the eventuality of my mother's death. I felt as though He wanted me to study the scriptures and learn as much as possible about the things He wanted me to know about death, heaven, and the comfort He could provide me as a believer in Him. In the early part of November, I began that mission. I again, started by researching the keyword death. I started a separate journal on November 11th to document all my findings. I read and copied each scripture I could find on the topic. I was thirsty to understand how my mother's impending death was going to affect both of us. The Bible is rich and fertile with information about death and how believers are to view it. It details why death comes to all and how it will affect a believer and their loved ones. It reveals how believers can attain comfort and courage in facing and dealing with the aftermath of death. God doesn't leave us emptyhanded with questions concerning the future of our beloved. Instead, He provides explicit details about what heaven will be like and the reasons we should rejoice in knowing our saved loved ones will spend their eternity there. After all, our lives here are but a mere vapor as seen in James 4:14 "Why, you do not even know what will happen tomorrow. What is your life? You are a mist that appears for a little while and then vanishes." With this journey being so temporary and fleeting, the assurances offered by God in loving preparation for the believer's eternal life in heaven brought a revived sense of renewal and hope to me. I was armed with the knowledge that God was preparing a place for my mother as affirmed by God's servant John

""

My Father's house has many rooms; if that were not so, would I have told you that I am going there to prepare a place for you? And if I go and prepare a place for you, I will come back and take you to be with me that you also may be where I am (John 14:2-3).

Furthermore, He promised me as a believer in Him, that I too would one day reunite with her after my journey here was complete. In many ways, it began to calm my fears and quell my emotional volatility. For the first time, I truly began to believe that my life, though all things old and familiar to me would change, would not have to crumble into a pit of hopelessness once she was gone. I was confident that He would bring me through the experience and enable me to run the race of endurance and become a conqueror on the other side of this loss.

CHAPTER 11

Finding Faith in Promises

There are few sure things in life, but death is one of them. We can all be assured that death will come to us at some point. Though no one relishes the thought of physically dying, it does become an aspect of this life that will confront each of us; some sooner and some later. God designates the length of time we are to remain in this life and no one except for Him knows that number. This truth is found in Psalm 139:16 "Your eyes saw my unformed body; all the days ordained for me were written in your book before one of them came to be" and in Job 14:5 "A person's days are determined; you have decreed the number of his months and have set limits he cannot exceed." Therefore, if I know that God is in control of my numbered days, I can live with confidence that He will also be in control of my destiny beyond my death. I know this because Paul writes "We are confident, I say, and would prefer to be away from the body and at home with the Lord" (2 Corinthians 5:8). Even Jesus told the thief next to Him on the cross in Luke 23:42-43 as the thief in his dying moments came to the realization that Jesus was in fact the savior of all, said to Him "Then he said, "Jesus, remember me when you come into your kingdom." Jesus answered him, 'Truly I tell you, today you will be with me in paradise." These biblical truths were serving to fill the void in my heart and soul as I was processing the idea

and subsequent emotions of my mother's impending death. I
needed something to cling to that would expel the emptiness
that kept invading me. A whirlwind of thoughts and feelings
pervaded me, and I vacillated between desperation to find any
method possible to prolong her life and acceptance of the
reality that she was moving towards her heavenly home. I
found that at times my thinking was quite irrational and
frantic, and it was only during the time that I spent in prayer to
God or studying His Word that my fears began to be allayed
and a quietness settled in my soul. I knew through His
teachings that as a follower of Christ, death was not an event
that was reason for anxiety or fear. Somehow, I had to bridge
the disconnect between my intellectual awareness and my faith
in God's promises. It is difficult at best being in the crux of an
emotional experience to maintain a rational perspective
because the humanness in each of us wants to lean toward our
own understanding of matters. Our intellect is limited to our
flawed existence and is based upon a narrow scope from a life
lived with blinders on. As a Christian, those blinders are
removed, and we can see ourselves and our world from a God-
given and life-sustaining perspective. Life given to us does not
cease once our bodies deteriorate to cessation; instead we are
then ushered into our eternal home where we can expect a
new life; one in which death will no longer prevail. I had
developed a strong faith in these assurances, and I wanted to
be armed with as much scripture as possible to have in my
arsenal as the time for handing my mother over to God
approached. The bible contains a plethora of knowledge
concerning death and heaven, but I want to share with you
those scriptures that I found to be particularly helpful and
encouraging to me during that time and equally since then.

It has been established that once a Christian ceases to

physically exist here in this life he or she is immediately in the presence of the Lord in heaven. Scripture informs me that when we die, we will be given new bodies as seen in Philippians 3:21 "...who, by the power that enables him to bring everything under his control, will transform our lowly bodies so that they will be like his glorious body." The ailments and afflictions that plague our earthly bodies will no longer hinder our heavenly bodies. We will immediately begin anew with bodies that reflect God's glory and will no longer suffer pains of any sort. We know that our bodies will be in a physical form as Jesus' was after his resurrection. It is illustrated in John 20:17 when Jesus told Mary Magdalene after she saw Him in His resurrected state "Jesus said, "Do not hold on to me, for I have not yet ascended to the Father.' It is also later seen when the resurrected Jesus is gathered again with His disciples and Thomas had previously disbelieved that Jesus had risen and was alive again. John 20:26-27 states

❝

A week later his disciples were in the house again, and Thomas was with them. Though the doors were locked, Jesus came and stood among them and said, "Peace be with you!" Then he said to Thomas, "Put your finger here; see my hands. Reach out your hand and put it into my side. Stop doubting and believe.

Equally as important is knowing that because Jesus was recognizable to His disciples after He rose from death, we too will be recognizable to those in heaven who have gone before us. The mere thought that I would be able to recognize my mother in heaven was greatly soothing to me. Her life in heaven no longer seemed to be an abstract idea. I was finally beginning to understand that heaven is a definitively physical place that exists, and just because I cannot presently see it or have some concrete physical connection to it in this lifetime, does not mean that it isn't real. My study of scriptures told me that heaven will be a gloriously beautiful place as seen in many areas of the book of Revelation. Revelations reveals an immense amount of information concerning the nature of heaven. John writes

"

Then the angel showed me the river of the water of life, as clear as crystal, flowing from the throne of God and of the Lamb down the middle of the great street of the city. On each side of the river stood the tree of life, bearing twelve crops of fruit, yielding its fruit every month. And the leaves of the tree are for the healing of the nations" (Revelations 22:1-2).

This is a bountiful description for believers to know that in heaven, every need will forever be met. But, perhaps one of the most profound scriptures that brought me enduring comfort was found in Revelations 21:4 'He will wipe every tear from their eyes. There will be no more death' or mourning or crying or pain, for the old order of things has passed away." Having watched the physical, emotional and mental deterioration of my mother over the previous three years, I had begun to long for her suffering to end. It was painful to watch, and I knew that her quality of life was fading. I had accepted the fact that there was absolutely nothing I could do to stop the progression of her illnesses, nor could I change the eventuality of her death. It had left me feeling quite helpless and even at times, hopeless. However, having discovered God's absolute truth about the believer's future beyond death, my fears and anxieties began to lessen, and I started to experience a renewed hope and sense of peace.

As Christmas day drew near, my mother's youngest brother learned that he had terminal cancer. He too was aged and decided to forego any type of treatment. Instead, he was sent home from the hospital with the services of hospice. My mother seemed to have a special bond with him as had been evident in the way she spoke so fondly of him through the years. In previous years, while he was still able, he came to visit her on a frequent basis, and they enjoyed each other's company immensely. I believed in my heart that the news of his illness was going to be yet another hurdle that she would have to overcome in the battles that had increasingly plagued her emotions as of late. Again, not knowing if her mental faculties as a result of the dementia would allow her to fully comprehend the nature and extent of his illness, I kept many of the details from her. I was finding that she was becoming incapable of remembering information that was presented to her on any number of given topics, therefore she would have to be reminded. When that happened, it was though she was reliving the experience all over again. I believed she intuitively knew that he was going to die because she would remark that he was the last living brother that she had. It was beginning to feel as though the last spark within her soul was becoming quenched. The fight within her was diminishing.

Christmas day finally arrived and after lunch, I took my mother to her home to begin the holiday festivities. All the remaining family members gathered that day and gifts were exchanged, and a wonderful meal was shared. One of her greatest joys through the years has been to watch the children unwrap their gifts. She had a special love for all children, and always sought to make them feel loved and special. That is one of the gifts that I received from her throughout my entire life that will always endure; the feeling of being loved. In the end, what could be more precious than to know that someone loved you with such depth and sincerity? Equally as painful, however, was knowing that after she was gone, no one would or could love me in that way again. But I was accepting God's Word in Ecclesiastes 3:1-2 "There is a time for everything, and a season for every activity under the heavens: a time to be born and a time to die..." Knowing that life and death are just a part of the cycle of seasons somehow served to take the sting from the pain I was feeling. Furthermore, I found great encouragement in 2 Corinthians 4:16-18 which says

"

Therefore we do not lose heart. Though outwardly we are wasting away, yet inwardly we are being renewed day by day. For our light and momentary troubles are achieving for us an eternal glory that far outweighs them all. So we fix our eyes not on what is seen, but on what is unseen, since what is seen is temporary, but what is unseen is eternal.

I knew God was telling me that though my mother was experiencing struggles at that time, and her body was giving way to death, I was to remain in my faith and hope for the glorious life that she was going to embark upon in her eternal destination. That brought me such liberation and freedom from the sullen mental anguish that came from dreading the loss of the one person who had always given me unconditional love and boundless encouragement the whole span of my life. The realization came to me that I was being selfish in wanting my mother to remain with me. I wanted nothing more than to preserve her and keep her with me for the duration of my lifetime; unrealistic, I know. I was discovering the grandeur that was to become her life once she was to enter the kingdom of heaven. I was inexpressibly grateful to God for His limitless love for both me and my Mom. To think that He loved us both so much that He wanted us to spend our eternity in His presence and with each other, was almost inconceivable. Though, admittedly, I cannot say that I understood that kind of love in all its entirety, I will tell you that I unequivocally believe it to be the absolute truth.

The Christmas celebration was quite taxing on my mother, and as days moved forward, I could see that more often than not, she was wearing oxygen and requiring the use of an anti-anxiety medication to calm her during bouts of labored breathing. The number of days were increasing when she would simply sleep aided by sedation, while I simply read and copied scripture into my journal. Those moments of quiet reflection in her presence are some of the most precious memories I have today of time spent with her. I could literally feel God's presence in that room. He was reassuring me of His awesome sovereign power and control. I had been praying for quite some time that when He decided to call her home that she would not experience any physical suffering. Ultimately, I knew that He had the perfect plan, therefore, I eventually learned to just pray asking for His will to be done.

The new year quietly entered our lives and I knew it would be the year that would forever change us both. Everything that I had been studying from God's Word and promises had become symbolically like placing pieces in the jigsaw puzzles that mom and I had spent innumerable hours completing; each piece, once placed in its correct location, brought us nearer to completion and enabled us to see the larger picture in more of its wholeness. So, it was for me with God's Word. The more I understood His promises, the more complete I was becoming and the better enabled I felt about my ability to endure the upcoming loss of my mom. I knew with certainty that I would never be fully prepared for what was to come because, humanly speaking, I have learned that those experiences are just that; moments in time that must be personally felt and processed. I knew I had to give myself permission to undergo whatever emotions and thoughts that were to come. But I too knew it was going to be vitally important to not allow those feelings to overtake my wellbeing. Ecclesiastes 3:4 states it so plainly in explaining that there is "...a time to weep and a time to laugh, a time to mourn and a time to dance..." I wanted to be able to rejoice after the mourning had passed and grief had played its part. I had every reason to delight in the future because I had the assurance that God would welcome my mother to her eternal home with open and loving arms and that she would never again have to suffer with pain, grief or illness. That thought alone brought me such great solace. I would, of course, naturally be sad surely for an indeterminate amount of time, but I was confident it would only be for a season.

By God's grace and mercy, January still contained days where Mom was still able to join me for lunch at a nearby restaurant and engage in some of her favorite activities such as bingo in her apartment. We watched western movies and old television programs which she enjoyed. Those things may sound simple and mundane, but they were experiences that I long for today but can never recapture. On January 24th, her youngest brother passed away, and as I anticipated, the news again brought sorrow and pain to her already agony riddled soul. The funeral was to be the following Sunday on the 27th and my husband and I were to take her to say her last goodbyes. When that day arrived, she inordinately struggled with her ability to breath. The medical staff had administered all the prescribed measures available to her and so I let her decide if she still wanted to attend the funeral. While waiting to leave for the funeral, I had my picture taken with my mother, which, unbeknownst to me, turned out to be the very last photograph that we would have taken together. Monitoring her condition closely, I kept inquiring if she felt able to endure the lengthy ride and sit through the service and she was adamant that she still wanted to go. So, armed with extra oxygen tanks and doses of other pertinent medications, we began our travels to the funeral home which had become an all too frequent journey for our family. We intentionally arrived early in order to give her an opportunity to have some private time alone with her brother; a chance to speak any words that had been left unspoken. I sat her wheelchair near his casket and watched in silence as her grief flowed forth and she appeared to be completely saturated with despair. Something deep inside of her seemed to change that day. I firmly believe that her willpower and determined resolve to keep moving forward in her life had begun to wane. Physically and emotionally, it seemed as though she had exhausted the fortitude necessary to sustain her innermost ability to resist the daily struggles she was encountering. On the ride back to the facility, I distinctly remember telling myself that I knew in my heart, that day would be the last ever that my mother would be able to leave the facility again. And, so it was.

As the family member who was the primary decision-maker for her, I found myself faced with the choice of whether to begin more frequent administration of the anti-anxiety medications to keep her calm and comfortable. Her breathing ability had deteriorated rapidly as I had been informed by specialist would probably happen because the overload of fluid in her body would eventually overtake her. When she struggled to breath, she became panicked which made her struggle worse. I sought God's guidance in this decision as I had learned to turn these matters over to Him. Never once did He fail to answer me. God showed me that I needed to be fully informed and directed me to meet with the hospice nurse and the director of the medical staff at the facility to discuss all the pros and cons of the increased frequency of medication usage. Upon gathering all the pertinent information, I made the decision to begin the medications on January 28th. I knew with certainty once the around-the-clock administration of the medications began, my mother would be in a state of unawareness from that point forward until God would send His angel to escort her to His kingdom. I found myself that particular morning telling her as often as possible how much I loved her, and she would always tell me she loved me too. Somehow, it seemed as though I could not tell her enough. There just didn't seem to be enough time. I knew that during all the time we had spent together those last two years, we had talked about everything conceivable. We had talked about our life together and often spoke of the fond memories of the experiences we had shared. We laughed about many things that life had sent our way. We cried together over sorrows and tragedies we had dealt with in our lives. We talked about what she preferred when it came time for her funeral; favorite songs and scriptures. Most importantly, we talked about her strong faith in and love for God. She said she wasn't afraid to die, and she absolutely trusted in God's Word when He spoke of receiving her into His heavenly kingdom. Though the thought of not ever again being able to engage in conversation with her from that point forward was debilitating to me, I also knew that truthfully, we had already spoken everything that we needed and wanted to say. What an honor and privilege it was to know and experience that. I never felt God's completeness more than I did at that time. I knew that He was bringing both of our lives full circle. She had given birth to me 53 years prior, and then I had become her pseudo mother and caregiver leading her home to God. My goal at that point was to keep her comfortable, help her to continue feeling loved, and remind her of God's love and eternal destination. I continued to find strength and comfort that God provided to me through His awesome Word. I knew with certainty that the separation between me and my mother would only be temporary because I was reminded in 1 Thessalonians 4:13-18:

""

Brothers and sisters, we do not want you to be uninformed about those who sleep in death, so that you do not grieve like the rest of mankind, who have no hope. For we believe that Jesus died and rose again, and so we believe that God will bring with Jesus those who have fallen asleep in Him. According to the Lord's word, we tell you that we who are still alive, who are left until the coming of the Lord, will certainly not precede those who have fallen asleep. For the Lord himself will come down from heaven, with a loud command, with the voice of the archangel and with the trumpet call of God, and the dead in Christ will rise first. After that, we who are still alive and are left will be caught up together with them in the clouds to meet the Lord in the air. And so we will be with the Lord forever. Therefore encourage one another with these words.

This scripture affirms that God will return for His children and faithful followers of His Son Christ Jesus. No one knows the exact date and time that will occur because only God Himself has that answer. However, He tells us unequivocally that upon His return, those who preceded us in death will rise first and then, if we are still alive at that time, we will be caught up with them in the clouds and taken to heaven to never be separated from our saved loved ones ever again. This was a magnificent assurance to me that I would be reunited with my mother one day in the kingdom of our Lord and would never have to endure being separated from her again. Furthermore, John tells me "I have told you these things, so that in me you may have peace. In this world you will have trouble. But take heart! I have overcome the world" (John 16:33). Also, Paul states in 1 Corinthians 15:26 "The last enemy to be destroyed is death." You see, death no longer has a stronghold on the believer. Therefore, it is not to be feared. These words were perhaps some of the most powerfully enlightening and comforting that I discovered during my time of need and I pray they too will comfort you.

CHAPTER 12

Living Completely Surrendered

Death was marching our way and there was nothing I could do to intercept it. As Monday the 28th progressed, my mother was slowly sinking into an altered state of existence because of the medication. She still had the ability to answer questions by nodding her head though her eyes were closed most of the time. She did awaken briefly for moments during that day and remained in a slight state of awareness even through that first night. I decided to remain with her with the only exception being to go home for a quick shower and pack a new bag on that first day. In the week prior, I had developed a sinus infection that eventually required me to make a trip to an after-hours express medical facility for medications that would hopefully contain the problem and provide enough relief to make it through the coming days. I knew that my body and mind were virtually depleted from lack of sleep and mental exhaustion. Even though the struggles were very real and searing, I knew that God was with me and would provide all necessary sustenance I would need to survive this season in life. The bible is filled with words written for our comfort and such words for me were found in 2 Corinthians 1:3-4

❜❜

*Praise be to the God and Father of our Lord Jesus Christ, the
Father of compassion and the God of all comfort, who comforts
us in all our troubles, so that we can comfort those in any trouble
with the comfort we ourselves receive from God.*

This one scripture alone would become part of the driving
force for this writing. I was to later learn that part of healing is
found in helping others who are also suffering.

As the clock continued its infernal tick, I found myself
reading back through the scriptures I had written and studied
just for the purpose at hand; to gain strength and comfort as
my mother was releasing her hold on life. It was as though the
words were my lifeline to hope; hope to survive the loss, to
endure the gut-wrenching pain of watching her physically
wither away, and to hold true to the promises that God had
given to me. I had written the scripture found in John 11:23-26
where Jesus was talking to Martha who was the sister to
Lazarus. Lazarus had died and upon Jesus' arrival, the scripture
reads

❜❜

*Jesus said to her, "Your brother will rise again." Martha
answered, "I know he will rise again in the resurrection at the
last day." Jesus said to her, "I am the resurrection and the life.
The one who believes in me will live, even though they die; and
whoever lives by believing in me will never die. Do you believe
this?*

Though Jesus was asking Martha, He was asking me also. Did I believe that by having faith in Him, my mother would never die? Yes, I absolutely did. I knew that Jesus was assuring Martha and me that as believers in Him, our saved loved ones may die a physical death, but spiritually, they will always live an abundant and joyous life with Him in heaven. Jesus did go on to raise Lazarus from the dead to show God's amazing glory to the people who were present that day, and through this biblical event, you and I would also know His power and might even today. I felt, in much the same way, that He wanted to show me this would not be the end for my mother. It would be the beginning of the most amazing everlasting life that she would ever experience. Comfort did abound within me when I thought of this. Furthermore, these words are found in the Beatitudes "Blessed are those who mourn, for they will be comforted" (Matthew 5:4). God confirmed here and in countless other books and chapters in the Bible that He would assuredly comfort me, not only through this difficult time, but also in all my afflictions.

In the weeks leading up to this time, I had purchased a book entitled *The Gift of Heaven* written by Dr. Charles F. Stanley. I greatly respect his work and when I was seeking a more in-depth understanding of heaven, I was led to that particular writing. It is a beautifully written and illustrated piece of work that speaks on many aspects of heaven and of our lives beyond this one with correlating scriptures to reference. Previously, on many days when Mom and I were inside bound, I would read to her from this book. It was very uplifting and inspirational. Unbeknownst to her, I suppose I was attempting to keep her mind filled with the beautiful images of heaven that God portrays in His Word. Perhaps in other ways, it was a method I was using to allay my fears concerning my expectations of my mother's upcoming departure for her new heavenly home. Either way, I believe it to be more than coincidence that this book by Dr. Stanley found its way into our lives and it would play a crucial role in the final few days I spent with my mother.

The staff at the facility where my mother resided was wonderful to her and gave her such loving care especially during her last days. We found that the next day brought about the same level of sedation that she had experienced the day before. She no longer was opening her eyes, but still seemed to have some ability to nod her head and mutter a few words when asked a question. A decision had been made by this time to discontinue all her regular medications since sustaining her life was no longer a viable possibility. The goal had become to keep her comfortable and to assist her in living her last days with utmost dignity. Something inside me would not allow myself to leave her. I was driven in my desire to stay with her at all costs. My sinus condition had worsened, and the medications seemed to have no effect on providing me any relief. I was unrelenting however, and by the grace of God, somehow was able to persevere. I had gotten very little sleep as my mind would not allow me to relax enough to physically shut down. I knew this season of suffering was only temporary and that God would enable me to run this race that had been laid out for me as long as I kept my focus on Him as seen in this passage "...And let us run with perseverance the race marked out for us, fixing our eyes on Jesus, the pioneer and perfecter of faith" (Hebrews 12:1-2). This was my race to run and I wanted to finish it well. The privilege of being able to be with her during the last days of her life and to still be able to physically touch her and talk to her was such a precious experience; one I'll always treasure. That Tuesday, the 29th, would be the last day that I would ever physically hear my mother tell me that she loved me. I had experienced many "lasts" that would fill the recesses of my mind and heart to carry me into my future without her. Truthfully, each day of our lives are potentially filled with these types of "lasts" because no one knows the number of their days to be lived in this lifetime. I'm still learning today to treasure the smallest of things.

Nighttime befell and in the still quietness, with only a dimly lit angel-shaped lamp next to her bed that was positioned near a picture of my father, I sat quietly beside her and merely watched what appeared to be a peaceful state of slumber. A lifetime of memories flooded my mind and at times, it was almost impossible to contain the emotions that welled inside. I truly believe that I had accepted the inevitable fact that life with my closest friend, confidant, and encourager was coming to an end. However, acceptance is quite different from enduring the raw emotions that naturally occur during such a critical life event. There were moments that I did not handle the process as gracefully as I had hoped but I knew enough to know that God understood every single emotion that tormented me, and I was confident that He was right by my side every agonizing second. During the night hours, I decided to read scripture to her. I had no way of knowing if she could hear the words, but if she could, I wanted her to hear my voice and be comforted by His Word. I began by reading John 14 to reassure her that our Heavenly Father had already prepared a place for her and would be coming back to take her to her new home in heaven. I wanted her to remember that as a believer in Christ and through His gift of salvation, she would begin her new life in His presence the moment He called her home. I wanted her to know that everything was ok. I had never felt so strongly the presence of God than I did during those moments. By this time, my mother had showed no indication of mental awareness since earlier in that day. What was to occur next still causes wonderment in me today. After reading John 14, I began to read from Dr. Stanley's book *The Gift of Heaven*. I was reading from the pages and talking to her about the content when suddenly, with her eyes still closed, my mother clearly asked me "Are you God?" I could barely believe what I had just heard and witnessed. I said to her "No Mama, I'm just reading some scripture to you." She nodded an acknowledgement and those were the last words I ever heard her speak. I will never in my humanness comprehend exactly what prompted her to ask me that question. I do often wonder if perhaps God was revealing Himself to her at that time. I'll never know the answer to that on this side of heaven, but I take great encouragement in believing that God was also with her and leading her home.

My mother remained in an unresponsive state for the remaining nearly two days. I had begun to notice the changes that were occurring physically and as a matter of physiology, I understood that time had become very limited for her. I had repeatedly prayed to God in the weeks leading up to her passing that He would not allow her to suffer and that when her time was done, that it would be a peaceful exit. Wednesday moved into Thursday and many goodbyes were spoken to her. I continued to sit by her bed and hold her hand or stroke her arm all the while talking to her about mundane and normal daily topics. I felt strong and I wondered why I felt that way. During a time when I should have been distraught and shattered by grief, I was instead calm and tranquil in my spirit. Undoubtedly, I can only explain this state of being as an act of the grace of God. He was indeed holding true to His promises to me by providing me strength, comfort, and endurance to navigate through the tangle of emotions and thoughts that He knew would certainly come. I repeatedly whispered in her ear that I loved her and told her that it was alright to let go whenever she was ready. At exactly 11:13 PM on Thursday, January 31st my mother gave up her spirit and went on to her eternal home in God's kingdom. I sat in my human disbelief and knew that she was no longer physically with me anymore. Her earthly struggles were finally over. She would no longer have to suffer from physical ailments, grieve the loss of her loved ones, or wonder what her life would be like beyond death because she immediately entered the presence of our loving Father and Lord. She was now in paradise in all the perfection that God had promised her. Finally, His will for her had become complete. Life was to be forever changed in ways I had even yet to discover. I didn't know what my future would hold in the coming days, months or years, but I was confidently sure that God had led me through these trials in life and He would guide me through anything that may lay ahead in my future journey.

The next several days were filled with the traditional functions in preparation for the funeral. As I picked out the clothes she would be laid to rest in, I recalled fond memories of the day we purchased them while on a shopping and lunch outing. I made sure that her favorite pieces of jewelry were among the items she would wear in the casket because I knew those things were special to her. I had prepared a list of her favorite scriptures and hymns that would be a part of her service. These things were important to her and I wanted to honor her wishes. I longed for her service to be nothing short of perfection. I went through the motions during the ceremony and, for the most part, was able to maintain a stable composure. In many ways, I had already grieved my mother's death long before she physically left her body. You see, I had been given the gift of time. And during that time, I had begun to clearly understand how God's plan had unfolded in such a way that He could accomplish His will and purpose in both mine and my mother's life in those last three years. He had granted me the ability to retire from my career and set into motion all of the necessary components that would enable me to, not only become my mother's caregiver, but to reap a bountiful trove of treasures in the form of memories and experiences that I would have never had otherwise. I am extremely blessed to have had the opportunity to give her the dignity, respect, and quality of life that she so greatly deserved. The strengthened bond between mother and daughter that was gained, the love we shared, and the memories we made, far outweighed any trials and struggles that existed during our time together. I came to understand that God gives each of us a purpose for our life and it is our responsibility to seek and discover His purpose and plan and to allow Him to guide us each day in its fulfillment. It is precious to me that God deemed me worthy enough to be selected as my mother's caregiver in the waning years of her life. There is no greater privilege, I believe, than to nurture the needs of a loved one and to bring loving quality to their numbered days. I have no doubt that when my mother entered the presence of God that He said to her "His master replied, 'Well done, good and faithful servant" as found in Matthew 25:21. She had lived a life that was honoring to God. She indeed was His faithful servant as seen through her love and compassion for everyone she knew. She exemplified the qualities that characterize our Lord like forgiveness, long-suffering, humility, mercifulness, generosity, and unselfishness. She was a truly genuine and inspirational person whom I feel so honored and blessed to have known as my mother and my friend.

I was sure that life without my mother was going to be painful at times, and the void left from her departure would cause deep aches for a while. I began moving forward with life taking each day as it unfolded. I had come full circle in my life through a sense of completeness that I had never experienced before. I realized that it had become necessary for me to have taken the path God had laid out for me. He had purposely led me through those three years of dark reign because He had things to reveal and teach me; things that perhaps I could not have discovered any other way. He used those dark times of trial and adversity to drive me to Him and show me that He loved me and wanted to be my all-sufficient loving God. He wanted me to lean on Him and His promises. I would not have known His promises had I not reached a level of desperation which resulted in an intense longing to search for answers, guidance, wisdom, and most importantly, hope. God made His bountiful eternal hope and comfort available to me, and as a result, I now live in a relationship with our Lord who is unconditionally loving and has taken the strongholds of darkness from my life. I live in the light of His ever-present grace and mercy. I wholeheartedly believe that we gain the most interpersonal growth during times of great tragedy or trials because in those times, we are better positioned to seek relief from the pain and heartache. Once we become seekers, then the door is opened for God to draw us into His loving arms and show us that this life was never meant for us to live apart from His strength and provisions.

Strife and disaster will always be a part of this fallen world that we live in. Each one of us are destined to be touched by troubles at some point in our lives; each on varying levels of intensity. Though the afflictions that are discussed in this writing were focused mainly on the role and responsibilities of a caregiver, truthfully, every person will have to endure hardships in their life regardless of the position in which they have been placed. It is my prayerful hope that the words presented in this writing and the scriptures revealed will bring hope to the darkness in your life regardless of your circumstances. There is power and strength in the Words of our Lord that certainly will illuminate any dark path that you may have to tread upon during your life's course. I speak with great conviction in telling you that if you will only reach out and seek the guidance from the only One who has all of the answers, He will guide you through the maze of figuratively dark tunnels that you may traverse and will empower you to successfully circumvent the obstacles that lie in wait for your arrival. I am thankful each day for the new perspective that I have been granted about life and its inevitable pitfalls. I am no longer a hostage taken by fear in waiting for the next major life event to cripple me. Surely, I know more crises are to come, but I am also certain that when they arrive, I will not face them alone. My faith and trust in God and the truth found in His Word guides and strengthens me daily. It is my fervent hope for you to discover the rich and bountiful relationship that awaits you when you become a seeker of God. He will never leave you in your times of distress. You and I have the incredible privilege of embracing the assurance that our loving Heavenly Father is always with us. There will come a day in our lives when that one promise will mean everything to us; it will be the day that the numbers of our days expire. Afterall, it is inevitable that death will come to us all. Personally, I am deeply grateful to God for revealing to me the means by which I could enter this loving relationship with Him. I came to understand that without salvation, there is no hope. And where there is no hope, there is no future. My faith in Jesus as my Savior has sealed the fate of my life forever; in this lifetime and the one to come. Jesus says there is no other way to reach our eternal life in heaven except through Him as He clearly says in John 14:6 "Jesus answered, "I am the way and the truth and the life. No one comes to the Father except through me." Because of this gift, I now live in quiet confidence and anticipation that when my days have elapsed, I will again be with my mother and will be surrounded by the perfection of God's love and I will never again endure loss, pain and suffering, nor will I be parted from her again. Human reasoning may question if this is true, but personally, I deliberately decided that I did not want to come to the end of my life and find out that I was wrong. It is my sincerest hope that through the trials and struggles of my journey, you may be encouraged to discover a faith-filled path devoid of fear with the reassurance that though darkness may reign at times in your life, you can live in complete confidence that light and hope is available to you as seen in the encouraging words in Psalm 119:105 "Your word is a lamp to my feet, a light on my path." My prayer for you is that you too will allow God to light the path in your life.

References

NIV – New International Version (2011)

The National Alliance for Caregiving (NAC) and AARP Public
Policy Institute (2015). *Caregiving in the U.S. 2015 – Executive
Summary*, pp. 9-13.

CPSIA information can be obtained
at www.ICGtesting.com
Printed in the USA
BVHW030205021219
565354BV00001B/80/P

9 781922 355638